THE TRANS-AUSTRALIAN WONDERLAND

A.G. BOLAM

With photographs by the Author.

ETT IMPRINT

Exile Bay

This 8th edition published by ETT Imprint, Exile Bay 2023.

First published in 1923 by McCubbinn James Press, Melbourne.
Reprinted 1923, 1924, 1925, 1926, 1927, 1978.

This book is copyright. Apart from any fair dealing for the purposes of private study, research, criticism or review, as permitted under the Copyright Act, no part may be reproduced by any process without written permission. Enquiries should be addressed to the publisher:

ETT Imprint
PO Box R1906
Royal Exchange NSW 1225
Australia

Copyright © this edition ETT Imprint.

Design by Tom Thompson.

Cover: "A real Australian Eleven, Natives Ooldeah"
 original photograph by A.G. Bolam, 1920.

ISBN 978-1-923024-02-1 (pbk)
ISBN 978-1-923024-03-8 (ebk)

To
NORRIS G. BELL
The First Commonwealth Railways Commissioner

A Wonderland of truly wondrous things
That nowhere else upon this Earth are found ;
Of reptiles rare, and birds that have no wings,
And animals that live deep in the ground ;
And those poor simple children of the Earth,
(A disappearing race you here may meet),
Whom whites have driven from their land of birth
To regions still untrod by booted feet

PREFACE

This little book was written amid the sandhills of Ooldea, and the matter in it is principally the record of my own observations and investigations; and what is not so has been extracted by me from the historical memoirs of this State, or has been supplied to me by the actual participants in the scenes and incidents which I now describe. Often, during my residence in this Trans-Australian Wonderland, I have thought that the experiences of myself and others who have been and seen would be of some little interest to those thousands of travellers who journey across Australia by the Trans- Australian Railway, and to whom that great railway is nothing else than a line on the map.

No college-trained naturalist am I, but a railwayman who in the odd moments when he has not been giving the right-away to trains, or taking down the tick-tack of the telegraph, has been taught his lessons in natural history by the greatest masters; of the subject - the blacks at Ooldea.

If this little volume should be regarded by naturalists as even an unimportant addition to the literature of the country, or if it be just of passing interest to the traveller by train, then shall I feel deeply honored. The writing of its pages has afforded me the greatest pleasure; but with that pleasure there comes pangs of pain when I reflect that the chief actors in the scene - the simple children of the scrub and the plain - are rapidly passing away to "the undiscovered country from whom bourne no traveller returns." With these black friends of mine crossing to the Great Beyond, is it a wonder then that Kendall's beautiful lines should ever be haunting my thoughts?

Will he go in his sleep from these desolate lands,
Like a chief, to the rest of his race,

With the honey-voiced woman who beckons and stands,
And gleams like a dream in his face -
Like a marvellous dream in his face.

The illustrations appearing in this volume are the product of my own camera, and the photos. have been secured in some cases. With no little ingenuity; for, although the blacks are somewhat partial to being snapped, the same cannot be said of the timid little animals whose home is round about this district or on the Nullarbor.

I cannot close this preface without thankfully acknowledging the services of Mr. John P. Monro, B.A., who kindly read through the manuscript, suggested improvements here and there, and saw this first edition through the press.

A.G.B, Ooldea, September 1923

PREFACE TO THE THIRD EDITION

The success of the First and Second Editions of the little book has far exceeded my most sanguine anticipations, and the appreciative letters received from Professor Wood-Jones (University of Adelaide), Messrs. L. Keith Ward (Government Geologist, Adelaide)., F. Garnett (Chief Protector of Aborigines, Adelaide), W. H. Tietkens (the Australian explorer), Norris G. Bell (Commonwealth Railways Commissioner), G. W. Card (Curator, Mining Museum, Sydney), John F. Connelly (Perth), A. J. Vogan (Archaeologist, Sydney), and many others; the very favorable reviews of many newspapers, magazines, and journals; and the knowledge that my little book has penetrated to the foot of the Himalayas, Cambridge University, Canada, United States, and other parts of the world; all these have emboldened me to essay a Third Edition, revised and enlarged. To those kind friends who have offered suggestions for the improvement of the brochure, or who have encouraged me in the pursuit of certain lines of investigation, I tender sincere thanks. The commendations of these gentlemen so eminent in the scientific world have firmed me in the resolve to know and to record accurately as much as possible of the vanishing aboriginals, the last of the Stone Age Men.

AGB, Ooldea, July 1924

PREFACE TO THE FOURTH EDITION

This Edition includes twenty-four additional pages of letterpress, and four illustrations. The additional matter consists of descriptions of other curious forms of insect and animal life, particularly the Trap-door Spider, the Pig Beetle, and the Circular-saw Grub. A considerable amount of interesting matter relating to the Aboriginals has been added. Several instances of tracking are recorded.

I thank my many friends for their kind appreciative remarks of my humble efforts.

A.G.B. Ooldea, August 1925

PREFACE TO THE SIXTH EDITION

The Fifth Edition was printed to the order of the New South Wales Department of Public Instruction for use in the Public Schools of that State; and this Sixth Edition is required to meet the popular demand.

I wish to express appreciation of the encouraging remarks contained in letters addressed to me by very many prominent people, and particularly by Messrs. Percy Grainger (the world-famous pianist), Frank Cotton (Ethnologist of Sydney), F. M. Forde (M.H.R. of Queensland), W. M. Garling (of Sydney), and the Rev. S. J. Kirby, B.A. (of the Bush Church Aid Society).

The inexorable requirements of the Department have necessitated my leaving Ooldea for Kingoonya; but I still retain a keen interest in my black friends and the charming fauna and flora of this country. I am hopeful of putting into print at a later date, some further interesting information.

A.G.B. Kingoonya, July 1927

CONTENTS

Preface 5

1. MAINLY GEOGRAPHICAL AND HISTORICAL 9
The location of the Wonderland - the gathering ground of the blacks for ages past – Venning and Howie Giles the Explorer's trip in 1875 – Tietkens's visit in 1878 – The meaning of Ooldea and Youldeh

2. THE SOAK 12
The only surface water for hundreds of miles – The Mecca of the blacks – The Curative Powers of the Bitter Well – The legend of Bug-in-jah and Car-bin-gee – All about the Fresh Water Soak –Its development by the Commonwealth Railways – Fresh, salt, brackish, and bitter waters found alongside each other – The water problem.

3. THE ANIMALS AND REPTILES OF THE WONDERLAND 19
A wonderland of animals and reptiles found nowhere else – The Marsupial Mole – The Kangaroo Mouse – The House-building Rat – The Crested-tailed Phascogale – The ordinary Bandicoot – The Rabbit-eared Bandicoot – The Pig-footed Bandicoot – The Dormouse Opossum – The White-footed Jerboa – The Dingo – Kangaroos and Emus – Other animals – The Mountain Devil – The Sleepy Lizard – The Racehorse or Cycling Lizard – The Frog or Barking Lizard – Goannas – The Fighting Spider – The Trap-door Spider – Scorpions – The Pig Beetle – The Circular-saw Grub.

4. THE BIRDS OF THE WONDERLAND 42
The Australian Wedge-tailed Eagle – The Australian Bustard or Wild Turkey – The Mallee Fowl – The Cave Owl – Many other birds.

5. THE VEGETATION OF THE WONDERLAND   48
Mulga and Myall – The Water-bearing Mallee – The Water-bearing Oak – Water in Trees – A Water-bearing Tuber – The Quondong – Spinifex – Buckbush – Saltbushes – Bluebush – Parakylia – Grasses.

6. THE NULLABOR WONDERLAND   54
The extent of the Nullarbor Plain – The world's longest stretch of straight line – "Nullarbor" means "No Tree" – An uplifted sea-bed – Immense animal life – The plain almost a true level – Blow-holes : The mystery of them – Enormous caverns extending for hundreds of miles – Dongas.

7. THE GEOLOGY OF THE WONDERLAND   61
Fossils – Diprotodon Australis – Limestone - Jasper, Tourmalines, and Garnets –The Mystery Stone or Skystone: Does it come from outside the Earth? – Brown Coal – The Possibility of Oil - Clay.

8. THE WONDERLAND CLIMATE   65
A perfect winter climate – Hot days, but cold nights – The rainfall – Extraordinary visibility – Fog – Rainbows – Heavy dews.

9. THE ABORIGINALS   68
Wild blacks see whites for first time – They deteriorate with civilisation – Wonderful in the bush – Blacks with the explorers – Original Ooldea Tribe now extinct – Blacks from North, East, South and West come to Ooldea – Social life – Their Wurleys – Food – Habits – Deaths – Burials – Sandals – Absence of chief authority – Bartering – Smoking – Marriage – Names of Off-spring – Weapons – Boomerang – Wommerahs – Spears – Shields – Tools – Native string – Whip-making – Water-carrying – Fire-making – Smoke signals – Medicine and surgery – Amusements – A threatened invasion – When black meets black – "Kings"– Shifting camp – Decorations – The right hand – Corroborees – Display for Prince of Wales – Sacred ceremonies – Message sticks – Writing – Ability to procure food – Tracking – Procuring water – Cannibalism – Character of the blacks – Extraordinary instances of reliability – Fidelity – Religious beliefs – Magic – Their lighter side – Appreciation of humor – A few black stories.

1

MAINLY GEOGRAPHICAL AND HISTORICAL

Ooldea is a station on the great Trans-Australian Railway that stretches 1051 miles from Port Augusta (South Australia) to Kalgoorlie (Western Australia). It is 427 miles from Port Augusta and 624 miles from Kalgoorlie; whilst it may be more exactly located in Lat. 30° 30' S. and Long. 131° 55' E. Ooldea is thus in the same latitude as Coff's Harbor, in New South Wales, and is on the same meridian as Darwin, in the Northern Territory.

Frequent travellers across "The Trans" speak of Ooldea as being on the edge of "the Plain." And so it is. The scrub country ends at Ooldea, and the great Nullarbor Plain commences there, and stretches west for a distance of 457 miles.

Ooldea has been the great gathering ground of the blacks from North, East, South, and West for many aeons; and one reason for its being so is the fact that it has always possessed perhaps the only place for hundreds of miles where a permanent supply of good water is obtainable. Some blacks at Fowler's Bay (125 miles south-east of Ooldea) boasted of this to Venning and Howie, two whites, who were well-sinking down on the coast, and conjured up so beautiful a picture that the well-sinkers took a trip out to the Promising Land. Of that trip no written record exists, as far as I am aware; but we do know that the great explorer, Ernest Giles, whose name is worthy of every reverence, when on his journey of exploration overland to Western Australia, was guided to the hidden hollow of Ooldea by Thomas Richards and a black named Jimmy, in 1875. Thomas Richards was a police trooper at Fowler's Bay, who had visited Youldeh previously, and Jimmy was a native of the district who, although upwards of 50 years of age when out with Giles, had been 100 miles east of Youldeh when he was a little boy. Giles intended to make Ooldea (or Youldeh, as he called it) the point of ultimate departure for the West; but before setting out on that perilous undertaking he went east to Sir Thomas Eider's station at Belfana, 450 miles away, where he was to obtain his camels. On the journey to Beltana, Giles and his party endured fearful privations; all their horses died from thirst, and the party were pulled through by the two camels which they had. Jimmy's unfailing knowledge of water-holes which he had visited about 40 years previously was the factor in conquering the first 100 miles, but after that the fate of the party was in the hands of the gods. Giles secured his camels at Beltana, took them down to Port Augusta, and left the Port on 23rd May, 1875, on his memorable trip to Perth. Ooldea was reached on 4th July; and on the 27th of that month Giles went westward from Youldeh on a preliminary excursion, whilst Tietkens and Young, two of his assistants, explored from Ouldabinna northwards. After these trial trips, the whole party assembled at Ouldabinna, and left that point on the 24th August for their plunge into the great unknown to Perth, taking their lives in their hands, and having to hold on to them with grim determination to prevent their slipping through. How the party fought its daily duel with death and won through, thanks to the "lion-hearted camels," the judgement of Tietkens, and the ability and loyalty of the black boy Tommy, is a glowing page in the history of Australian exploration. Those who care to do so-and all Australians should - may read the account in Giles's *Australia Twice Traversed*. W. D. Cornish, of the Surveyor-General's Department. Adelaide, went to Ooldea in 1876, and it would appear that he is responsible for the change of the spelling from "Youldeh" to "Ooldea."

    W.H. Tietkens, who was second in command of the Giles expedition in 1875, returned to Ooldea in 1878, and struck out northwards. He sank a well to a depth of 122 feet, in the hope of striking good water, and of thus being enabled to open the country to the Musgrave Ranges, 280 miles away. Brackish water only was obtained, and Tietkens's Well, 35 m. north of Ooldea on the map of Australia, marks the first and an heroic attempt to open up this country, and it still stands as the only effort. H.Y.L. Brown, the Government Geologist, was at Ooldea in 1885 and again in 1897, and a few other Government officials saw the place in subsequent years, but from 1909 until Furner, the South Australian railway surveyor, put his pegs into the land at Ooldea and on the Nullarbor, no white man penetrated the solitude; and but for the great railway, which followed on those pegs Ooldea would have remained the two-foot deep waterhole of the blacks, these pages would never have been written, and the natural history of Australia would have been the poorer.

The name "Ooldea" is aboriginal, and means "a meeting place where water is obtainable." The Ooldea tribe of blacks is extinct; those now about the place are blacks from other parts. But the oldest of them pronounces the name as though the spelling were "Youl-dee" or "Youl-deh"; and this latter spelling was the one adopted by Giles, and shown thus on his maps.

Once upon a time – in the year 1917 – the name of the railway siding, then known as "Ooldea," was approved to be altered to "Deakin," so as to fit in with the intention of the then Minister to call the stations on this Commonwealth Railway after the Prime Ministers of the Commonwealth, and these names, commencing with Barton (376 m. from Port Augusta), ran in the order of the Ministries: Thus the name "Deakin" should follow "Barton"; then come Watson, Reid, Fisher, Cook, and Hughes. The name "Deakin," in accordance with this arrangement was applied to the station at 427 m., and which up to then was known as "Ooldea." It would have been a great mistake to have obliterated the name of "Ooldea" from the map, on account of its historical interest; and "the powers that be" evidently realised this, for the reign of "Deakin" lasted just over two months, when "Ooldea" was reinstated to its rightful place, and "Deakin" was shifted on 172 miles to just across the border, thus destroying the proper sequence of Prime Ministers. But what of that?

2
THE SOAK

Across the 1051 miles of the Trans-Australian Railway one may search the surface in vain for even a thin thread of running water, although nearly 2000 miles of coast-line run more or less parallel to the steel road. Yet the rainfall of that country averages about 8 in. per annum, but it falls as a rule in heavy showers distributed throughout the year. The area of this country is so vast that the volume of water represented by one inch of rain is simply enormous. The water runs generally in a southerly direction, and then is gradually absorbed by the loose soil or the spongy lin1estone until it vanishes. Whither goes this vast volume of water? Ah! that's for the future to disclose! But it seems certain that great reservoirs of water are to be located in the underworld. Anywhere on the plain water can be obtained by boring; but it is of variable quality; in some cases being potable, in others good enough for stock; but in several instances it is unsuitable for any purpose owing to the salt contents. One is sure to strike water on the plain at approximately sea level, and in a great many cases at a higher level than that of the sea.

But this chapter concerns the Soak. In three known places in Sub-Central Australia, the underground water indicates its presence by appearing at the surface. The places are: (a) the foot of the cliffs at Twilight Cove, where surface springs exist; (b) the Queen Victoria Springs; and (c) the Soak at Ooldea.

The Soak at Ooldea has been known to the blacks from time immemorial. For century upon century it has been the gathering ground of blacks from North, East, South, and West. They went there to perform their sacred ceremonies, their corroborees, and their tribal customs. They congregated at that place to barter their spears, boomerangs, wommerahs, shields, clay, etc., for goods or weapons of other tribes. The sick and the injured made a pilgrimage to Ooldea to partake of and to bathe their wounds in its wonderful waters. The armorers of the tribes for hundreds, probably thousands, of years, brought their flints, grinding stones, and other materials to the Soak to employ the intervals between the ceremonials in a profitable occupation. Each wind that blows uncovers these relics, but covers others.

In the days of the blacks two soaks only were known, one being fresh water and the other bitter. It was the water from the latter that had the reputation among the sons of the soil as the great cure-all for skin diseases, internal complaints, and wounds. The bitter well is only two chains away in a north-easterly direction from the fresh water well known as "The Soak," from which it is separated by a slight rise, and it is surrounded with a green water-weed. The weed is found only in this hollow, and it grows thickly to a height of about five feet. The fresh-water soak known to the blacks is situated in the middle of another hollow, and is over-looked by a very barren sandhill, running in a half-moon shape from the north-west; and it is in the centre of salt and bitter water country - a spot where one would least expect to find fresh water. The Great Architect in His infinite wisdom so ordained that a permanent water supply should be located in the midst of desolateness and barrenness.

But the blacks say that many, many moons gone by, Bug-in-jah, the water man, who lived far away in the Musgrave Ranges, had a water bag made from human skin, and filled it with the precious fluid from a spring in the ranges, and then set out to establish a sacred ground for the tribes. In the course of his journey he met Car-bin-gee, who, in the form of a small animal, followed him, and persistently requested a drink; but Bug-in-jah, being bent on a most important mission, refused to allow him even a mouthful of water. Car-bin-gee, nevertheless, followed in his tracks, getting

The original Soak amid the sandhills at Ooldea. A Gathering Ground for the Blacks for Ages. Giles camped here in 1875.

The Ooldea Railway Station, 1920.

worse and worse as the days dragged on, and imploring the water man for a drink. Bug-in-jah still refused, and after journeying many days he came across a spot suitable for his purpose, and planted the water-bag underground. Car-bin-gee, now perishing from thirst, and angry at the loss of the water-bag, attacked Bug-in-jah, and a fierce fight ensued, in which Bu g-in-jah was badly injured and Car-bin-gee killed. Bug-in-jah, being severely wounded, was able to plant only a little water, and at a very shallow depth, and this he did at night lest anyone else should see him do it. Bug-in-jah then lay down in a quiet place, and his life ebbed away. He thus sacrificed himself, in order that fresh water might forever be obtainable in the sandhills by his people. And that is the reason why the wells at Ooldea Soak to-day take up to 24 hours to fill, and the water is only three feet below the surf ace. So say the blacks.

Ooldea being a place sacred to the blacks and the rendezvous of the tribes from near and far, was known to all aboriginals; and some blacks at Fowler's Bay told Venning and Howie, who were well-sinking in that locality, of the country – wonderful to them – lying up in the north-west. These whites, typical of the pioneers of the past, journeyed 130 miles out to see the promised land, and came to the Ooldea Soak: They saw a small hole about two feet deep with water in it; and as fast as they used the water the supply was renewed. They returned to Fowler's Bay, and reported what they had seen. The next of the whites to see the Ooldea Soak was Trooper Richards, of the S.A. Police, whose duty called him to that remote locality; and the next were Ernest Giles, the great explorer, whose guide to the hidden hollow was an aboriginal, and Giles's assistants, Tietkens and Young. This was in 1875. Mr. Tietkens, in a letter to me, regarding the Soak, states:-"In 1875, when there with Giles, it was a hole two feet deep. We had about 20 camels, so we deepened the hole, and put an ordinary case down to keep the sand back." Tietkens returned to Ooldea in 1878, and found the Soak just as he had left it three years before. He, however, whilst using Ooldea as a base, pushed north, with the intention of opening up the country to the Musgrave Ranges. The attempt failed, and Tietkens withdrew, but he left his name on the map of Australia in Tietkens's

Well. The next white to visit the Ooldea Soak was H.Y.L. Brown, the Government Geologist of South Australia, who visited the place in 1885, and, under instructions from the Commissioner of Crown Lands, carried out a geological exploration of that region in 1897. Accompanied by Surveyor Murray and two men, he reached Ooldea with eight camels on 1st May. Brown, in his report, stated: "Ooldea Wells is the only known reliable and permanent watering-place in this region"; and in another part he remarks: "The vegetation and the various kinds of bushes at this place are most suitable for camels, which, having plenty of water and food, commenced to improve in condition after the first day's rest." The camels had travelled 234 miles from Ooldea outwards and back without water! In 1901 J. G. Stewart, a Government Surveyor in South Australia, passed through Ooldea when examining the country from Tarcoola to the W.A. border, in connection with a proposed railway. He reported that the soakage well at Ooldea had a sufficient supply to be of service during construction. R.T. Maurice also explored this country in 1901; and in 1904 F.R. George was sent out from the Department of Mines on an examination for minerals, and to report upon an alleged discovery of gold by prospectors. Mr. Henry Deane, who visited Ooldea in June, 1909, found that the well, which was 28 feet deep, contained a good supply of water. The actual original well of Giles and later explorers has since caved in, and a peg now marks the historic spot.

But the Commonwealth Railways Department has improved the water supply at Ooldea beyond recognition. In the first hollow below the sandy ridge, there are now seven wells, all connected, and from which water is pumped to the railway siding to meet the domestic needs of the railway employees and their families for more than 100 miles each side, and for locomotive supply. Further on is another engine-house and a batch of good wells; and then close handy are wells containing salt, brackish or bitter waters, unsuitable for loco. requirements, but quite good enough for stock. About half a mile from the first wells and engine-house No. 1 is the last batch of wells containing good water, and these, too, have a pumping plant. Altogether, nearly 50 wells, with an average depth of 15 feet, have been tried, and of these 19 give good water, which is pumped to the siding daily, the quantity piped being approximately 4,000,000 gallons per annum. Some of these wells take over 24 hours to replenish. Probably if more wells were sunk in other locations the supply of good water would be augmented considerably. It is only within the last three years that the Soak has been drawn on to any extent, and during that time there has been no deterioration in the quality or quantity of the water.

The soakage comes from a north or north-easterly direction, and possibly originates at the Musgrave Ranges (280 miles) or Everard Ranges (235 miles). A heavy rain, just distinguishable on the horizon in the north or north-east from Ooldea, will benefit the Soak in a few days or a week, depending, of course, upon how far away the fall occurred. This fact prove two things - that there is an underground flow, and that the flow is from the direction of the ranges towards the Southern Ocean. The water is found flowing over the top of a clay bed, and the clay is covered with sand in depth varying from three feet to 15 feet. One of the most marvellous things about it all is that, within a few hundred feet, and in the same barren, sandy patch, fresh, salt, brackish, and bitter waters should be procurable. These waters are all obtainable from the same level, viz., the top of the clay bed.

The Soak is a wonderful asset to the Railways, because it is a permanent water supply in a country where a surface reservoir cannot be built owing to the sandy and porous nature of the soil; and there is no loss from evaporation, which in an open reservoir on this line is equal to 12 feet of water per annum.

Clays of various colors-white, yellow, brown, and violet – are obtainable, and they are of a soapy and slippery nature, lending themselves readily to modelling. Models made by hand and baked in an oven become exceedingly hard.

The water problem of Sub-Central Australia is a difficult one. That there is a fair annual rainfall is known; that not one drop of the rain reaches Mother Ocean by the surface is also established; that the rain is absorbed by the sandy or light soils and the limestone is indisputable; that water caught in the dongas escapes into caves has been proved. If, then, these underground rivers or lakes can be located and the water brought to the surface and turned into irrigation channels, it would not be surprising to find the countryside favored as it is with a splendid climate and protecting scrub-covered ridges – smiling with vineyards, orchards, vegetable garden and lucerne plots.

3

THE ANIMALS AND REPTILES OF THE WONDERLAND

There is nothing more interesting than a study of the animals found in the Ooldea district, for many of them are peculiar to the country, and are beautiful little creatures. In the sandhills of Ooldea and on the Nullarbor Plain several rare specimens of the smaller mammals are found. Many of these mammals have, in older settled localities, either become extinct, or are rapidly becoming so. According to the blacks, there are other animals further north which are unknown to the whites, and which are indigenous to that part, or have been forced further back by the advent of the fox or other foes. Those with which I am familiar, and of whose habits I have made a close study, are the Moles, Kangaroo Mice, House-building Rats, Fat-tailed Mice, White-footed Mice, Phascogales, Bandicoots, etc. etc. I give hereunder a necessarily brief description of a few of the most interesting animals.

THE MARSUPIAL MOLE - The Mole or Blind Sand Burrower (*Notoryctes typhlops*) is known to the blacks as Arra-jarra-ja, and is probably the most wonderful marsupial inhabiting this country. Being a pouched animal, it carries its young in much the same manner as the kangaroo does. The Mole is about six inches long, and has a beautiful, soft, fine fur of a creamy color. It has no eyes, and there is no trace of its ever having had any; and no ears, or, at least, no outward indication of any. The front legs have five digits, two being relatively enormous claws, two others being smaller, and the fifth is practically a horny boss or rudimentary part. The back legs have webbed feet, but they also contain five digits, three of which have small claws, and one is a rudiment.

The Marsupial Mole has for a tail a small sinew three-quarters of an inch in length, marked with a series of encircling rings, with a horny knob at the tip, and when the animal is moving above the ground, the sinewy tail is used as a fulcrum, and it leaves a trail in the sand. This Mole is an extraordinarily fast burrower, the two strong claws on each front leg enabling it to excavate at a very rapid rate, whilst with its webbed hind feet it pushes away the sand very rapidly. All four feet work almost simultaneously, the fore ones and the nose cutting into the sand, and the back feet forcing it up into the space behind. It can burrow vertically, and after being seen on the surface it will completely disappear in a few seconds, and leave no indication as to the direction in which it is travelling. Having no eyes (which apparently are not required in its underground life), the Mole is not handicapped by going down to a great depth. It appears on the surface only after heavy rain, and when there it crawls a few yards, then burrows down and re-appears a few more yards away, crawls two or three yards, then down it goes again; but it does not crawl far or live on the surface for any length of time. In hot weather it apparently goes down very deep, as it seems to be unable to stand the heat, and it cannot tolerate strong light. This little animal has never been known to emit a sound of any kind, not even when cruelty has been applied. It is, therefore, blind, deaf and dumb. But if it lacks those senses, it makes for the deficiency by possessing an acute sense of smell, and is very sharp in its movements. As far as is known the Mole lives on underground insects and ant eggs; but attempts to keep it in captivity on such a diet have been unsuccessful, probably owing to a want of appreciation of the fact that it needs darkness. It does not resent handling, so apparently it is not fear that is accountable for its dying in captivity, as is stated by some scientists. The Mole, however, is a nervous little animal, and gives proof of that fact in a most remarkable manner. In a feverish haste it will make tours of its cage; round and round it will go until suddenly it will drop off to sleep quite unexpectedly, and it will just as suddenly wake up, and off it will rush again. It will even fall asleep in the middle of a meal, then wake up with a start, and with the utmost speed devour what is left. Nothing is known of the breeding habits, or of the young of this remarkably interesting animal, and this feature the scientists are very eager to have information about. In all probability the female Mole lives in a deep burrow, where it produces its young far removed from the possibility of attack by foes. During the excavation of the railway cuttings in this district the workmen came across the Moles on several occasions.

THE KANGAROO MOUSE. - The Kangaroo Mouse (*Hapalotis mitchelli*), known to the blacks as Ool-git, is found well distributed all over the countryside. He is a pretty little fellow, and derives his scientific name from the Australian explorer, Sir Thomas Mitchell, who was the first to describe him. This little chap resembles a kangaroo, having two long hind legs and two short fore ones. He stands on the hind legs, and, although no bigger than the ordinary domestic mouse, he hops along at an incredible speed - so fast, in fact, that a good dog cannot overtake him. He hops three feet at each bound, and can continue to do so as long - as pursuit lasts. His endurance is wonderful, considering his size. A tail of about six inches in length, with a fine brush at the end, is a distinguishing feature. The Kangaroo Mice live in burrows, which are very cunningly constructed, a peculiar feature being what is commonly known as the dummy hole. A burrow is started, and all the earth is very carefully scratched out at the one and only opening. To do this work two mice are generally employed, one behind the other; and, when the front mouse starts burrowing, the other one, which is immediately behind, scratches the dirt away. As might be imagined. the pair are Mr. and Mrs K. Mouse, who are building a home for themselves; and each takes a turn at burrowing into the sandy patch which is situated on a rise. As the excavation progresses, one or two holes make their appearance some distance away from the original opening, and, strange to say, no earth is scratched out at any of the new openings, but it is all taken out at the first entrance. When the burrow is finished, the original hole is completely blocked up by the dirt which has been stacked outside, and it is used no more. In the course of time, this dirt is blown away or covered over with leaves, and assumes a very aged appearance. This is just what the mice want, as the ground, being so obviously unused, is passed over without notice. The holes, therefore, become very difficult to detect; and a small opening of three-quarters of an inch, in all probability under a bush, is the only entrance to their underground home. Unless he has a knowledge of the habits of these lovely little animals, or he is a good tracker, the naturalist will pass over and over their burrows and not be aware of the fact. The blocking up of the original opening has another purpose of greater importance, and that is, if the enemy is digging them out, and is approaching success, the mice will burrow through the original opening, which they had previously blocked up, and make off. Their homes are fine examples of strategic construction which our military engineers might copy to advantage. The Kangaroo Mice, when trapped alive, can be kept in captivity, and will live on a vegetable diet. They are easily tamed, and being such lovable little fellows they become great favorites as pets.

THE HOUSE-BUILDING RAT. - Another born architect is the House-building Rat (*Conilurus conditor*), which received from the blacks the name of Bal-gool-ya. It is remarkable for the fact that it builds for itself a wonderful home of sticks, and yet it has a burrow underground. The house is built of fine sticks, and these are so placed that they withstand the onslaughts of fierce winds. Frequently I have come across houses in which stones have been intermingled with the sticks. These stones, which are from one to one and a half inches in diameter, have been placed by the House-building Rats in among the sticks to give the structure a solidity sufficient to withstand the gales or the assault of enemies. Generally the homes are located under low tree branches, or in isolated hollows against some kind of shelter, and they are built of various dimensions, the usual size being about three feet in diameter and two feet in height. One large house that I examined measured six feet in diameter, and was four feet high, compact, circular in shape, and tapered to the top, where the diameter was one foot. It was constructed of grass, leaves, stones and small sticks. On the "roof" a pair of brown hawks had built their nest. In the interior, two feet above

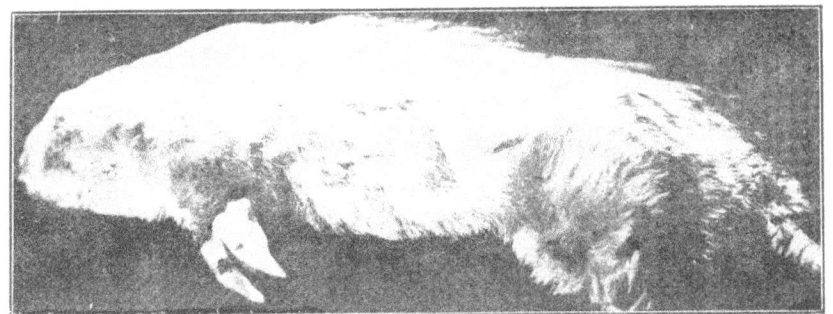

The Marsupial Mole: A Most Curious Animal, Blind, Deaf, and Dumb; but a Remarkably Fast Burrower.

The Kangaroo Mouse (top) and the Rabbit-eared bandicoot, or Bilbey.

the ground, was a nest, in which there were young. The nest was made of grass, very fine sticks and leaves. Towards the exterior of the building, the sticks were comparatively large, and it is marvellous how such small animals could place them in position. Each year the original home was added to, so as to accommodate the young people who brought their wives or husbands home; and so, in the course of years, the house is built larger and larger. Unlike many other small animals, the House-building Rats live all together in one colony, and one nest and burrow may house quite a large number of individuals. The young rats perform the building operations, and make the additions as they become necessary, whilst the old ones supervise only. In placing a large stick in position, they are just like so many workmen, and there is in all probability an old rat as boss. They usually start work at dusk, and the greater part of construction is, therefore, done in the darkness. The building is not constructed to an architectural plan, but, like many a white man's home, it is put up piecemeal, and to suit the requirements of the growing colony. Immediately under the nest, in the centre of the ground floor of the house, there is an opening, which connects with their underground burrow, and this is used by the mother as desired. The young are born in the nest, and are kept there until they are able to use the burrow for themselves. In the ground there are many holes leading into the nest, and connecting with the underground burrow (situated, as stated above, in the centre of the nest, which had been built immediately over the opening). The House-building Rats breed very quickly, and the young grow very fast. A peculiar habit of this animal is the carrying of the young attached to the teats, as is the case with some other animals of the Marsupialia. The young are attached with great tenacity, and do not become detached until about nine or ten weeks old. Another peculiar habit is the giving of a danger signal, and this is done by the animal striking the ground with its tail. Like most rodents, the House-building Rats have a fondness for sweet things, which they relish when in captivity. Table scraps they are specially fond of, and on these they live and thrive when captive. Nevertheless. in the wild state, they are strict vegetarians.

THE CRESTED-TAILED PHASOOGALE. - This animal, which bears the scientific name of *Dasycercus cristicauda*, is known to the blacks as Mul-garra. Two species of the Phascogale family are found on the Nullarbor Plain and in the sandhills of Ooldea. These are the Crested-tailed and the Brush-tailed; but, with the exception of a small difference in the hair on the tail, the species are alike in appearance and habits. They are carnivorous and have been known to kill smaller animals, rabbits, and birds. On one occasion a young Phascogale, about six inches long, was unwittingly placed in a cage beside a full-grown rabbit. To our great surprise, on the following morning, we found the rabbit dead and the young Phascogale asleep upon the body. It seemed incredible that such a small animal could attack and kill a full-grown rabbit; but when an examination was made we found that the Phascogale had fastened on to the rabbit between the ears, and had then eaten through the rabbit's head, thus killing it, and after sucking the blood it had fallen asleep upon the body. The young of Bandicoots, House-building Rats, Mice, etc., are easy prey for the little Phascogale, which not only catch them when out feeding, but raid their homes and cause great slaughter. In periods of drought the Phascogales and foxes create havoc among the timid animals. Although the Phascogales are so blood-thirsty, they do not fight among themselves. In fact, they are affectionate to one another, and will lay their heads on each other as they bask in the sun. These little creatures have learnt to appreciate the value of, and the security afforded by, a somewhat larger opening adjoining their own burrows, for the latter are invariably placed on top of a rabbit warren. This apparently affords greater safety than the open bush country, and it certainly makes their capture a very difficult thing; whilst it has the third and undoubted advantage of being close to a plentiful supply of excellent food. A peculiarity of their burrows is the perpendicular entrance. This entrance is usually a small hole about an inch in diameter, and descends perpendicularly for from anything up to three feet. For this reason it is a very difficult matter to dig these little animals out, but they are easily trapped with a piece of fresh steak as a bait. Another peculiarity of these most interesting animals is their habit of snuggling up close to each other in cold weather, each lying on top of the other (like "sacks in the mill") with only the head of each to be seen, excepting, of course, the body of the uppermost one. The object is undoubtedly to promote warmth. The young attach themselves to their mother's teats with remarkable tenacity, but should they become detached at an early stage in their existence, they will die. When they are a month old, however, it is possible to re-attach them by hand, and likewise this is probably so in their wild state. When a Phascogale, with five young attached, was being photographed, it got away being unaccustomed to the surroundings. Hither and thither it ran, backwards and forwards over all manner of boxes and other obstacles, but, after considerable trouble, it was finally recaptured with the five young still attached. Her movements were in no wise restricted by the load she carried - which appeared to be no handicap whatever - and not one of the young became detached, although the mother became exhausted and eventually died. In captivity, these little animals are quite fearless, and show a remarkable discrimination in dealing with food. For instance, an ordinary live domestic mouse will be instantly killed and devoured, but a piece of raw steak will be pulled about and carefully smelt until they are satisfied all is well. A curious feature about their feeding habits is the way in which the front paw is used to pick up small beetles and such like. Insects which are too small for the mouth to grip are smartly picked up by the paw and conveyed to the mouth.

BANDICOOTS. - The Ooldea sandhills and the Nullarbor Plain abound in various species of the Bandicoot family, the principal varieties being the ordinary Bandicoot (*Perameles myosura notina*), and the Rabbit-eared Bandicoot (*Thalacomys lagotis*), otherwise known as the Bilbey, Pinkie, Dalgoo, etc. A new species of the Rabbit-eared Bandicoot was recently discovered in this district, and was given the name of *Thalacomys nigripes*. It resembles T. *lagotis*, but is a little smaller, the fur is a darker fawn, the fur underneath more silvery, and the ears are exceptionally long. Like the other Bandicoots, it relies more on its wonderful hearing than its eyesight for locating its food.

There are several other species of the Bandicoot in this district but they have not been definitely identified. A few years ago these remarkable little animals were to be seen all over the countryside; but, with the advent of civilisation and its destructive weapons, and the ravages of the fox, the Bandicoots are being rapidly exterminated. Time was when these animals themselves could be seen, but with the increase of their foes those that remain have become timid, and the only indications of their existence that one sees to-day are the well-known pig-rooting marks where they have been digging for food, and these are gradually getting scarcer. The Bandicoots belong to the Marsupialia, and they carry their young in the pouches from the embryo stage until they are fully capable of looking after themselves. The pouches in these animals differ from those of other marsupials, inasmuch as they open in the opposite direction. Bandicoots live on all kinds of grubs, insects, vegetable matter, roots, etc., and they are particularly fond of a large wood-boring grub called the Bardy (Zangera). The Rabbit-eared species is much larger than the ordinary Bandicoot, and has a very fine steel-blue fur and a long tail, with a white tip. All species of Bandicoots live underground in burrows, which, in outward appearance, resemble rabbit burrows, but there are no runs or bolt holes, such as are usually associated with rabbit warrens. The Rabbit-eared species show great skill in the construction of their homes, and so much so that it is almost impossible to dig them out. The burrow, after going a yard or so, gradually turns into a circle, and continues one circle under the other, each getting deeper and deeper as the burrow progresses. The burrows are not entirely free of cross-driving, but are nearly so. The Rabbit-eared species also frequently make their homes in rabbit burrow, and apparently they live in complete harmony with the rabbits. Tracks of the Pig-footed Bandicoot have been seen and followed to its burrow (a rabbit warren which was impossible to dig out), but no live specimen has been captured as far as the writer is aware. Bandicoots of various kinds can be kept in captivity, but attention must be paid to a few essential matters. In the first place extreme care must be exercised to ensure that they do not quarrel among themselves, as they fight so viciously that they kill, and even the victors will be damaged so severely that they will subsequently die. Again, warmth must be supplied, because the animals are greatly affected by climatic changes. And as they only appear at night it is necessary to keep them in a dark place, because they are so timid that the slightest noise will frighten them, and, being unable to see well in the strong light, they will crash against the sides of the cage, and kill themselves when frantically endeavoring to escape.

DOORMOUSE OPOSSUM (*Dromicia conrinna*). - This is a very pretty little animal, being a beautiful faun on the back, with a yellow coloring underneath. One was caught at Fisher, right out on the Plain, and up to the time of its discovery it was not thought that the animal would travel so far from the timber country. The morning was cold when I received the little fellow, and it had rolled itself into a small ball, which, when pushed, would turn over and over, and after being forcibly straightened it would roll up again and assume the attitude of sleep. It has a long tail, by which it could cling to any suitable object and hang therefrom. The Dormouse Opossum is about the size of an ordinary mouse, with a tail four inches long; and its distinguishing features are the sharp head, thin large ears, and large eyes of the opossum family. Its fur is thick and soft. A beautiful little animal.

BUSH MICE or WHITE-FOOTED JERBOA. - These little rodents, which bear the scientific name of *Pseudomys hermansburgensis,* are distributed over practically the whole of the district round about Ooldea. Like nearly all other rodents, they live in burrows, which, for animals so small, are very large. One burrow which I measured carefully was 19 feet 3 inches in length, 11 inches deep at its greatest part, and had seven dead ends and one nest. Under ordinary conditions the Bush Mice are most sociable, and several families will occupy the one burrow, but at breeding time, each pair separate and make a home for themselves. They build a round nest of about six inches diameter, usually with two openings, and the nests are made of grass, small sticks, etc., outside, and of fur and other material inside. They breed freely and quickly, with usually four young at a birth. The sociability of these little animals is much appreciated by snakes, which make fearful inroads upon the little colonies.

THE DINGO. - One of the most important of the larger animals is the Dingo - important from the necessity of destroying it wherever possible. The Dingo is fairly common through the whole countryside, both on the plain and in the sandhills. If you watch out of the train when crossing the Nullarbor you will probably see a Dingo trotting along a few hundred yards away or sitting close to a rabbit warren awaiting his morning or evening meal. Its sense of smell is extraordinarily keen, and when on the hunt it never barks or makes a noise, but stalks its quarry rapidly, and seldom misses. On moonlight nights it reaps its harvest. The extermination of this pest is a necessity if the country is to be stocked with sheep. On Wirraminna Station alone the dingoes a few years ago killed no less than 16,000 sheep. The name "Dingo" is said to have originated with the blacks, who applied it to the dogs of the early settlers, but their own dogs - the real wild dogs of Australia - were called "Warrigals." The early settlers, however, applied the term "Dingo" to the wild dogs, and it is now generally accepted as applying to all native wild dogs. Dingoes are of different colors; for instance, there are white, yellow, brown, and black dogs, and the natives have different names for each. They do not, as is generally supposed, regard the yellow dog as the pure Dingo. The majority of the dogs now caught are crossed; and these crossed are by far more cunning and savage than the pure bred, and if run to earth or trapped, they will fight strenuously. They are more powerfully built, show a greater disregard for the white man, and frequently hunt in twos and threes. They are of various colors, and somewhat resemble tame breeds, but have more stumpy ears, and shorter and more rounded noses. The true Dingo, unlike the wild dogs of other countries, does not hunt in packs, and is seldom seen with another. A Dingo is commonly supposed not to bark, but to emit only a dismal howl, which he gives vent to at night, and is answered by other dogs if in the vicinity. On one occasion, however, a trapped Dingo snarled at its captor, and several cases have recently been noticed out here where trapped dingoes have emitted a low barking sound. This tends to confirm the theory that some Dingoes acquire a feeble bark from hearing the domestic dog, or the noise may be nothing else than the remnant of the bark that the Dingo's ancestors possessed thousands of years ago, when they crossed from Asia to Australia.

KANGAROOS AND EMUS. - These representative Australian animals are still to be found in the Ooldea district, and particularly on the Nullarbor Plain portion of it. Naturally, one does not see them from the train, but if one were to visit the vicinity of the rock-holes or the dongas out on the Plain, one would find Kangaroos and Emus fairly plentiful. Right out on the plain near the 130th Meridian there still remain some iron tanks under a small galvanised-iron shed erected right back in the 'nineties by a kangaroo shooter named Batt. It is to be hoped that the Nullarbor Plain will ever be a sanctuary for these animals.

OTHER ANIMALS. - That other typical Australian animal, the Wombat, lives in this land; and, unfortunately, those imported pests, the Rabbit and the Fox, flourish. Rabbits are particularly numerous, especially in a good season, and the Dingo has a great time. The Fox is causing great havoc among our native fauna - Turkeys, Bandicoots, Moles, and other animals fall easy victims to his wiles. This curse in Australia is of very recent advent to the Trans-Australian Wonderland; but it is multiplying at an alarming rate, and the sandhills are covered with their tracks. No less than seven were trapped here in a week recently, and it is evident that the time is coming when this pest from England, like the Sparrow, will have overrun the continent. They seem to expand together, but the Sparrow is a rara avis in this part. Away to the north, where very few whites have ever ventured, and where the Fox has not yet exploited, there are animals new to science, according to the descriptions of the blacks who frequent those parts. Here, then, is a great field for the naturalist to investigate, and with the railway at hand, and supplies of food and water so easily procurable, now is the time to get to work and ascertain what wonders are still hidden away in the great unknown. The Australian Museum in Sydney sent quite recently a collector into the Nullarbor country, and he went home laden with treasures obtained in this part. The collections made by these men confirm the opinion that many Central and Northern Australian mammals have worked their way down south to the Great Australian Bight.

REPTILES. - Snakes and Lizards are in goodly numbers. Snakes of a species unknown elsewhere exist; and quite recently a Death Adder (*Acanthopis pyrrhus*) was procured, and although Adders of this kind were first obtained by the Horn Expedition into Central Australia, it was never thought that they would be found so far south as Ooldea. Of Lizards there is an almost infinite variety, but four call for particular attention.

THE MOUNTAIN DEVIL. - Among the extraordinary lizards of this wonderful country, the most curious is the Mountain Devil (*Moloch horridus*), one of the most formidable looking animals of the Reptilia, yet one of the most harmless. The Mountain Devil is anything up to a foot in length and is simply one mass of spikes. Its head and brain in particular are specially protected by a large bump consisting of two horns, and from the resemblance in this respect to his Satanic majesty, the animal derives its name. On the neck there is a very pronounced fleshy excrescence, something like a knapsack. It has been suggested that this excrescence is an extra food storage for hibernation; but it is not so, for it has been proved that the knapsack is simply a solid lump of tissue. In my opinion, the excrescence is provided by Nature as a false head to deceive the birds which are the enemies of the Moloch. This lizard has a habit of putting its head down, and whilst its head is so bent the knapsack resembles the head, and birds would attack it in mistake for the head, and without any harm. Resulting to the Mountain Devil. This little ani mal is armored for defensive purposes only, and is accordingly quite capable of holding its own against other lizards or lizard-eaters of the neighborhood. It realises that it is practically immune from attack, and

A Mountain Devil in its home in a cave. Note the eight eggs.

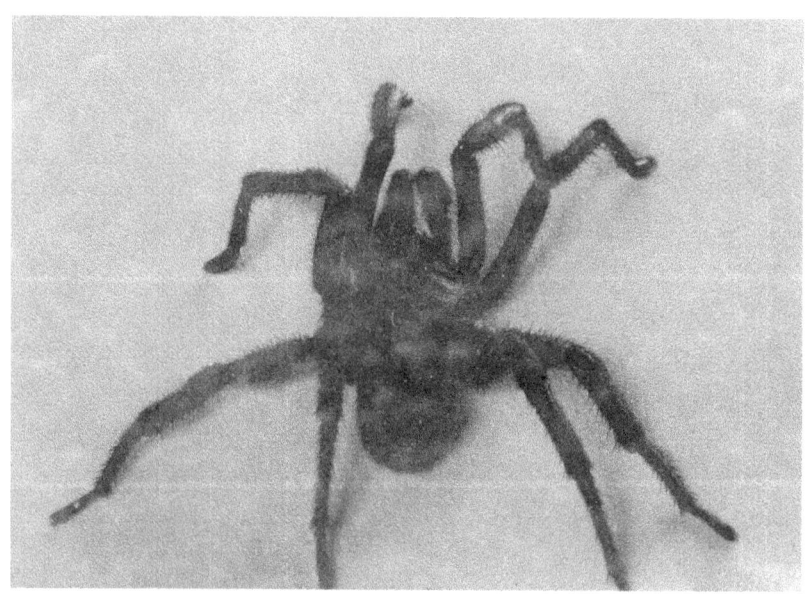

A big Black Fighting Spider, life-size.

consequently, it basks quite openly in the sand patches. It frequents the driest and sandiest soils in this tract of country. "Defence and not Defiance" would be a suitable slogan for the Mountain Devil. The illustration herewith shows the Mountain Devil and eight eggs laid in line upon some sand. It lays from 8 to 10 eggs in November, and they are about half an inch in diameter, 2 in. to an inch in length, with a tough leathery skin. These eggs are soft-shelled, and must on no account be exposed to strong light even for a minute or so, otherwise their fertility would be destroyed. The eggs are laid in a sandy patch, and are immediately covered, and left to hatch for themselves, like the eggs of its heavily armored and giant distant relation, the Crocodile. Like the Chameleon, this reptile possesses the power of changing its color in a remarkable way, so as to harmonise more or less with the colors of the objects about it. It also changes color when its temper is ruffled. The Mountain Devil makes a nice pet (although so repulsive-looking), and as it lives on flies and ants, it's "a handy thing to have about the house." It is estimated that this lizard eats as many as 1,000 small black ants at a meal. After breakfast it takes a little constitutional walk.

An interesting feature about the Mountain Devil is that it does not drink through its mouth, but absorbs the water through its body, just as a piece of blotting paper would soak it up. If the Mountain Devil is placed on a hot day in a tray of water, very soon moisture will be visible on the upper portions of the skin, it having been soaked up through the animal's surface in contact with the water. It is assumed from this that it ordinarily obtains its moisture from dews, and perhaps from the damp sand in which it burrows.

THE SLEEPY LIZARD (*Trachysurus rugosus*). - This curious reptile is known also as the Stumpy Tail Lizard. It is notorious for the sluggishness of its movements, and forms a remarkable contrast with the Racehorse Lizard, described hereunder, and which also inhabits this Wonder-land. The Sleepy Lizard moves along at almost a snail's or tortoise's pace, and, consequently, has great difficulty in getting out of anyone's way - particularly if it is crossing a track upon which vehicles run. It is a hideous but quite inoffensive reptile, dark brown in color, with yellow spots, whilst its belly is greyish, with brown spots, and its palate is black. Its body is round and thicker than a man's wrist, and the length of it is anything up to 18 inches. It sleeps generally all day, and is very difficult to rouse into any state of "activity," even a good hard kick from a man failing to produce an effect. When once roused, however, it can show fight, opening its jaws very widely, and if it should bite a person the effect will be very severe. The Sleepy Lizard is insectivorous. This lizard is also called appropriately the Shingle Back.

THE RACEHORSE OR CYCLING LIZARD. - This extraordinary Lizard is called by the blacks "Due-all." Scientifically it belongs to the Agamidae family, and is of the genus *Amphibolorus caudicinctus*. It is a fair-sized lizard, growing to about 15 inches in length. The front legs are small, but the back ones are very large, and the tail is long, and has circular stripes around it. It runs at an incredible speed (hence it receives the name of "the Racehorse"), and the movement of the back legs bears a remarkable resemblance to the motion of a cyclist (from which fact it is appropriately called The Cycling Lizard). When the Lizard is feeding or moving about, two inches of its tail is used as a support, which leaves quite a distinct mark on the sand; but when excited or in flight, the lizard raises its tail high above the body. Chasing the Racehorse Lizard is to the blacks what coursing is to the whites. It is no uncommon sight to see a score of young blacks enjoying the sport of chasing one of the lizards, and if one may judge from the shouts and roars of laughter, the diversion causes great amusement and excitement. The Racehorse is too speedy for the blacks, and too elusive for their sticks and stones. This lizard is of a hibernating nature, seeking the seclusion of a burrow in which to spend the winter months. In the spring it emerges from its winter quarters, and about November the female lays her eggs, and as many as eight are found in the nest. In size, these eggs resemble those of pigeons, but the ends are more round ed, and the shells much softer (as is usual in the case of the lizard family), and, again, as is usual with nearly all other members of Reptilia, the eggs are hatched by the heat of the sand in which they are deposited. It resembles the Mountain Devil and the Chameleon in its ability to change its color. When I caught one recently it was quite red around the head, but after being in a box for a few hours the red had changed to black, and the white rings around the tail had become a grey. The change in color was very pronounced. The Racehorse or Cycling Lizard is a very timid fellow, quite harmless, clothed in many colors, lives principally on flies, and, as is the custom of his race, enjoys a hot sunbath. To know him is to love him.

THE FROG OR BARKING LIZARD. - This is an extraordinary lizard, and from the fact that when teased it opens its mouth and barks, it is also known as The Barking Lizard. The blacks call it "Coor-a-bin." It belongs to the Gecko family. From the illustration, it will be seen that the head portion particularly of this lizard bears a remarkable resemblance to a frog. It has the large eyes, the identical mouth, the same frontal formation, etc., and on this account, it has been named the Frog Lizard. Perhaps it is the connecting link between the families of the frogs and the lizards in the great scheme of Evolution. Ordinarily a quiet fellow, but when teased considerably its fighting qualities are fully aroused, and it will then raise its front feet from the ground and make vicious little snaps. When thus teased it emits a sound which is likened to a bark, and for this reason it is known also as the Barking Lizard. The blacks find a certain amount of amusement in making this interesting creature bark. When teased it will invariably raise its body, and lift its front feet off the ground, open its mouth and snap, all the while emitting a sound resembling a bark. The habitat of the Frog Lizard or Barking Lizard is generally a blowhole or some other dark or covered place, such as under a log or the bark of trees, etc. Its length is about five inches, and in color it is usually a combination of yellow spots and black markings, with white on the underpart. The older lizards develop small spines, but they are very minute, and, unlike the Mountain Devil, the spikes play no part in Nature's scheme of defence, as in the younger lizards they are entirely absent. Like the Mountain Devil, it is insectivolous, and is a splendid fly-catcher. As the illustration shows, the Frog Lizard has a peculiar fat tail, which is used as a prop. The tail is easily broken off, but when that occurs, no harm is done, for another one soon grows. Indeed, it is not an uncommon thing for these Lizards to be found with two tails - the old, damaged one and the new one growing. When the new tail reaches maturity, however, the old one falls off. A very interesting feature about the Frog Lizard is that when attacked it has the power of casting off its tail; and the cast-off tail jumps about, thus diverting attention to it, and enabling the Lizard to escape. Note also the crinkled skin on the underpart of the body and tail. Truly an extraordinary animal.

GOANNAS. - These giant Australian lizards inhabit the Wonderland, and attain a good size. I have seen a few about four feet long. At one time I had as a pet a fine large Goanna (*Varanus gouldii*), whose home was in the hollow of a tree close by. Every meal time this pet would come to the door of my camp and await his meal, which consisted of scraps of nleat, bread, etc., thrown from the table. "Joe" was a very good scavenger, and he saw to it that no bits of food lay about the camp, and frequently he would be found in the dirt tin. A neighbor, who was a fettler, and a bachelor, had some fowls very well bred and good layers. On returning home from work at the close of each day the fettler visited the fowl yard to reap his harvest of eggs, but repeatedly he found the nests empty. Suspicions were cast upon his mates who lived close handy, and accusations caused a good deal of unpleasantness. One day I heard a great commotion in the fowl yard, and decided to make an investigation. To my surprise and dismay there was my noble "Joe" having a furious fight with the rooster. Standing off he would rush the rooster and grab him by the neck, tearing off mouthfuls of feathers at a time, until the rooster had none left. The bird was bleeding profusely, and looked as though he were done for. It then became necessary to do for "Joe," and a well-aimed shot effected the purpose. On the post-mortem it was found that the goanna's stomach contained three eggs, shells and all, badly broken, dozens of large maggots alive, some blowflies, and scraps of meat.

The Monitors of this species (*Varanus gouldii*) are, generally speaking, very useful reptiles, as they keep in check rabbits and other pests, but, unfortunately, they have a penchant for fowls and eggs. They live in burrows of their own construction, or in hollow logs and trees. When disturbed they make for the nearest opening, and frequently run down rabbit burrows or up trees.

The blacks use the oil made from the fat of goannas for healing sores and for anointing the hair.

THE FIGHTING SPIDER. – One of the largest spiders in the world is found in the Wonderland. It is the Fighting Spider - a big, black chap, four inches in length - which is notorious for its pugnacity. With the least provocation, or with none at all, it will attack man, beast, bird or reptile, and woe betide the victim it bites. The photographic illustration is life-size; and the reader will agree that it is "some" spider.

THE TRAP-DOOR SPIDER. – Amongst the small creatures the Trap-door Spider ranks, I should think, as the greatest of the home-builders, for he is architect, excavator, carter, plasterer, joiner and painter. The construction of his home demands hard work and patience, and when it is completed it resembles more a palace than a house. The Spider is careful in the selection of suitable soil in which to make his home. Having chosen the site, Mr. Trap-door commences to excavate, and the spoil is carted away for some little distance, and scattered by him so as to leave no indication of the locality of his house. The excavation consists of a tube about 3/4 inch diameter, and as he progresses Mr. Trap-door lines the walls with a silken web in just the same way as the tunnel for the underground railway in Sydney is lined by the constructors. A depth of about 10 in. is usually excavated, and the bottom is slightly larger than the tubular entrance. When the excavation is completed, Mr. Trap-door gives the walls a second and heavier coating of silk; and that done he attaches a wonderfully-constructed door at the entrance to his home. The door is fastened to the lining of the walls by silken hinges, and, being accurately made by a master joiner, it fits the mouth of the tube exactly. The outer covering of the door is finally smeared with a material the colour of the surrounding soil, and this renders Mr. Trap-door's home very difficult to find. When Mr. Trap-door enters his home, he closes the door behind him, and when he goes out the door is left open. Although he is so careful in the construction of his home that it is very difficult to locate, Mr. Trap-door unfortunately cannot devise a means to def eat the keen sense of smell of his deadly enemy, Mr. Bandicoot; and this keen sense revealing to the enemy the whereabouts of the Trap-door Spider, the Bandicoot digs down alongside the burrow to the bottom, and devours Mr. Trap-door in his home.

SCORPIONS.-These are found in the sandhill country, and when a person is sleeping out in the open he has to be very careful to see that there are no Scorpions' nests round about. The Scorpion is nocturnal in his habits, but a light or a fire has a peculiar attraction for him. As the sun goes down, and trees, houses, etc., cast their longest shadows over the face of the earth, the Scorpion issues from his burrow in search of food. He travels with his two large pincer-like claws in front wide open and in readiness to grip the unfortunate beetle or other insect that may happen to be in his way. The claws are covered with hair, which act as feelers, and immediately the feelers come in contact with anything the claws close quickly upon the victim and hold it down while the flexible tail of the Scorpion bends over and injects some poison into the prey. The tail is armed with a sting which is so sharp that it will penetrate a piece of cardboard, and through this sting the Scorpion ejects his poison. Human being, are not often stung by this creature, and when one is stung it is very rarely that fatal consequences ensue; nevertheless the sting is very painful, and immediate attention is necessary. The female Scorpion lays eggs, and when hatched the young are carried on her back for the first week of their existence, and thereafter they scamper off and look out for themselves. Beetles, crickets, flies and even small lizards and similar creatures form their food. It is said that Scorpions do not sting each other, or if they do they are immune from the poison; but nevertheless they fight each other, and when one is killed he is eaten by his conqueror. Married ladies and gentlemen will be interested to learn that Mrs. Scorpion usually kills and eats her husband.

I was fascinated once by a battle royal between a Scorpion and a large Red Striped Spider. The fight lasted a very short time, but was a deadly encounter. The Scorpion manoeuvred around the Spider, who stood up in a fighting attitude watching every move of his belligerent opponent. A sudden thrust by the Scorpion, and in the twinkling of an eye the Spider was thrown upon the back of the Scorpion, who attacked the enemy most viciously with his spiked poisonous tail, whilst the Spider endeavored to penetrate the Scorpion's scaly back. The soft body of the Spider was penetrated by the Scorpion's sting, and gradually the Spider weakened, and he was soon at the mercy of his victor, who would undoubtedly have made a meal of him if my collecting bottle had not interposed.

On another occasion I was out collecting, and came across a young Scorpion which I gathered up and thrust into a box wherein I had previously placed a big Centipede. Hearing a scratching noise shortly afterwards, I opened the box, and found a mortal combat proceeding between the large Centipede and the small Scorpion. There was no means by which I could unravel the numerous legs of the two opponents entwined around each other, so I simply had to let them fight it out. Getting out of the box, they rolled over and over upon the ground, appearing to us nothing else than a ball of fine legs woven into each other in all directions. For quite a time they fought on, neither relaxing his grip so far as we could see. Rolling over and over, twisting this way and that, they never relaxed the grips, but fought on and on until they died in each other's legs. Thus ended a fight to the death, with neither the victor. The Scorpion was a young one, whilst the

Centipede was mature; but whether a full-size Scorpion would have produced any different result, I am unable to say.

THE PIG BEETLE. - On hot summer nights we are frequently visited by Beetles which bear so remarkable a resemblance to a pig that they are aptly termed Pig Beetles. The arrival of the Beetle is announced by a very pronounced buzz, and a thud as it strikes a wall, and another as it falls to the floor. The Pig Beetle has two large horns, or spikes, over the rear portion of its head, and two smaller ones immediately over the narrow front of the head. It has a small rounded snout about one-sixteenth inch in diameter, on each side of which two long antennae protrude; and above these there are two black eyes, which are very large in comparison with the size of the Beetle. I give an illustration of the Pig Beetle.

THE CIRCULAR-SAW GRUB. - An extraordinary insect inhabiting the sandhills is an elusive sand burrower of the genus Cylindrodes, known to Science as the "Mole Cricket," and to the blacks as "Mirrin Muckoo," but colloquially called by us out here "The Circular-saw Grub." As it moves along on the surface this insect makes a raised seam of sand which sometimes extends to a couple of chains; and it is impossible to ascertain from the trail in which direction the Circular-saw Grub has gone, for the raised seam gives no clue. The method adopted by us is simply to dig at one end of the track, and if the object of our search isn't there, we try the other end, and the insect is generally found enjoying a rest. The actions of this insect are intensely interesting to observe. Whilst on the surface it can either advance by means of its centre legs (which in motion resemble the caterpillar wheels of a "tank"), or it can move backwards by the same agency. But it is ever seeking a place in which to burrow; and the little centre "caterpillar wheels" - of which it has two on each side of the body - are used to advance or reverse in its endeavor to find a suitable place to burrow. A remarkably interesting feature of the insect is the possession of two small circular saws with sharp teeth. These saws are situated one on each side of the head, and are perhaps more oval than circular shape. They are about ¼ in. long, $3/16$ in. wide, and $1/32$ inch thick; and they work up and down at any angle desired, sawing a tunnel for the insect to get along in, the little caterpillar wheels propelling the heavy rear portion. To assist the action of the saws the head portion of the insect turns, as if upon a swivel, in any direction desired, thereby allowing the cutters great freedom of movement. The tracks of the Circular-saw Grub are usually found running from the top to the bottom of a railway cutting in the sand; and it was quite a long time before I ascertained the origin of the curious little sand ridges; but one of my black friends explained it to me and gave me a lesson upon the habits of this most extraordinary insect. The accompanying illustration does not adequately represent the wonders of the Circular-saw Grub.

The Racehorse or Cycling Lizard.

The Pig Beetle.

The Curcular-Saw Grub.

4

THE BIRDS OF THE WONDERLAND

Equally as interesting as the animals and reptiles, are the birds of the Wonderland. These birds range from the smallest of wrens to the world's biggest bird of flight-The Australian Wedge-tailed Eagle.

THE AUSTRALIAN WEDGE-TAILED EAGLE. - This monarch of the air attains an enormous size out on the Nullarbor Plain, measuring in some instances 12 feet from tip to tip of outstretched wings. The Eagle builds a nest that a man could sit in without discomfort. These fine birds are also the victims of civilisation; and strychnine and dingo-traps are claiming their toll. Being carrion eaters they live on live animals and pick up the baits laid for dingoes; and thus we frequently find one caught in a trap. The strength of the eagle is remarkable. I have seen one of these birds which had dragged a loaded dingo-trap weighing at least 20 lbs. some hundreds of yards. On another occasion an eagle which had been caught in a weighted rabbit trap dragged the impediment across rough country for over two miles, then having got rid of the weight flew off with the rabbit trap still attached to its leg. I read in the *World's News* recently where an eagle had been caught in Scotland with a rabbit-trap attached to its leg. Was it my bird? Eagles attack rabbits and other animals, and their wonderful vision and great speed and weight make them formidable and almost invincible enemies to all forms of animal life. On one occasion, the piteous squealing of a rabbit attracted the attention of a passing man, and on approaching to investigate as to the cause, he saw a large eagle about to fly away, and a squealing rabbit running backwards and forwards. He caught the rabbit and found that both its eyes had been completely picked out by the eagle, which had held it down for that purpose. The eagle is a savage bird at any time, but it becomes very ferocious when its off-spring are young. It can be kept in captivity, however, and when well fed on meat, scraps, etc., it grows to an enormous size.

THE AUSTRALIAN BUSTARD. - There is probably no more stately bird than that magnificent specimen of the feathered tribe known as the Australian Bustard (*Eupodotis australis*), but more commonly called the "Wild Turkey" or the "Plain Turkey." The "Turkey" is a fine big handsome fellow, and as its diet consists of caterpillars, grasshoppers, and pests of that kind, it is a valuable bird. Despite the fact that it is protected the whole year round, it is ruthlessly destroyed by so-called "sportsmen." It is a fine sight to see a flock of 20 or 30 of these birds slowly rise, and make off in stately procession. Before rising, the "Turkeys," being heavy birds, are compelled to take a few steps to get the necessary impetus, and this serious drawback often results in their destruction. When flying they have to keep their wings moving, for immediately the wings stop the birds glide to earth. They cannot volplane like an eagle or a hawk. Never more than one young one has been noticed with its mother, and it is, therefore, presumed that only one chick is hatched at a time. Like Quail, the young Bustard leaves its nest almost as soon as it is hatched, and wanders over the ground secure in the protection afforded by the similarity of its feathers with the surrounding vegetation, until its wings are developed sufficiently to permit of flight. When feeding or resting, the "Turkeys" always have scouts on outpost duty, and if danger draws nigh, the scout is the first to rise, emitting a peculiar squeak as he does so. The rest immediately follow. These birds are very inquisitive, and their attention is consequently easily attracted by any unusual sight. The blacks know this, and in stalking a "Turkey" an aboriginal will often disguise himself to take away the form of a human being. Without some disguise, it is almost impossible to get close to them on foot, but a man on horseback or in a buggy or a motor car can usually approach to within a close range. Even a train can get within a comparatively short distance of these birds. I know of a case of a Bustard which was caught when young and retained in captivity. It was reared on hard-boiled eggs, and grew into a very large and strong bird. It was apparently quite contented in domesticity and made no attempt to escape. It followed its owrler about just as a big dog would do, and being very playful, the bird became a great pet. Perhaps one of these days, it will hear the call of the wild and "go bush," to fall a victim to "the nullah, the sling, or the spear," or the gun of the "sportsman." It would be fair game to the black who knows not the game laws, but not to the white, who should know the laws of the game. In one district alone in Western Australia, 184 Bustards were killed in one month a few years ago. In good seasons "Turkeys" become very numerous. Every day we see flocks flying across. In one flock I counted 28 birds; and when out driving one evening recently we rose 56 at different places.

THE MALLEE FOWL. – The Mallee Fowl (*Leipoa ocellata*) or Lowan is also found in the Ooldea District, where their peculiarly constructed nests and remains of others are more frequently come across. Of the four mound-building birds of Australia, the Mallee Fowl is the only one inhabiting the dry portion of the Commonwealth, and it is rightly regarded as being one of the most unique birds of the world. It belongs to a genus that has made Australia zoologically famous, inasmuch as it arranges for artificial heat to incubate the eggs in a mound of sand and decomposing leaves. Some of these mounds have a circumference of 48 feet.

The Mallee Fowl derives its name from the fact that the bird is always found wherever the Mallee or similar scrub exists; and mallee country is mostly sandy and has a small rainfall. These birds are very shy, and are rarely seen. Their gait is a slow walk, although they can run fast if necessary. The nesting part of the mound is made of leaves, bark, twigs, and vegetation. This is wet by the rain, and the egg are then laid and are placed upright by the hen, which then scrapes around them. The eggs are laid in tiers. When all the eggs have been laid, both birds build up the mound by scraping the sand together with both feet and wings. The heat of the decaying vegetation and the sand hatches the eggs, and the parent birds open the nests for the chickens to emerge. The old birds seem to take very little notice of their young, and the latter have to "scratch for themselves" from their birth. They are well able to do that, being strong and well-developed, and they can fly a short distance. But they trust to their running and hiding to escape danger.

Unfortunately, these fine birds, like many other of our feathered friends, are being forced further afield into the unknown country as civilisation advances. The question has been recently raised as to whether the Mallee Fowls can live without water, and that query has been prompted by the fact that their nesting mounds are found as much as 15 miles away from the nearest known water. Being that distance away, it is certain that the birds do not fly to the water, inasmuch as they are very poor flyers, being like the domestic hen in that respect. They probably get the necessary moisture from dew-laden leaves, etc. The eggs of the Mallee Fowl (or Mallee Hen, as it is frequently called) are brought in by blacks during the season. In size and flavor, they compare very favorably with the eggs of geese. During Giles's terrible journey from Boundary Dam to Queen Victoria Springs in 1875, Tommy, the black boy (whose discovery of the Queen Victoria Springs among the sandhills undoubtedly saved the lives of the whole of the party, and the camels), brought in some Mallee Fowl eggs, and these were very welcome when the larder was so depleted. Again, between Queen Victoria Springs and Mount Churchman forty-five Mallee Fowl eggs enriched the wanderers' larder.

THE CAVE OWL. - As its names implies, the Cave Owl makes its home in the caves and blowholes of the Nullarbor Plain. The ledges that project from the side walls of the blowholes form favorite nesting places for these curious birds. The Cave Owl is a big bird, with snow - white feathers, but its face is ringed all round with light brown feathers, and there is also a sprinkling of brown on its wings. There is a wonderful expression conveyed by its large eyes and brown eyebrows. I shall never forget the expression of anguish in the eyes of a dying Owl which had been shot; it was really wonderful. The Cave Owl appears only at night, and in the moonlight it presents a beautiful sight as it perches on the limestone rock or some small scrub on the edge of the Plain. This species of the owl tribe is probably confined to the Nullabor.

The Owls used to be seen almost every night, but as they caused havoc among the chickens the shotguns had to be used upon them and they are now rarae aves.

OTHER BIRDS. - A description of the various birds which frequent the Ooldea District would necessitate a volume itself; but space permits of only a passing reference to the many kinds. In addition to those dealt with above - and, of course, the Emu, which I have coupled with the Kangaroo in the previous chapter - there are Blue and White-shouldered Wrens, Red and Black-backed Wrens, Black and White Caterpillar-eaters, Short-billed Tits, Babblers, Chatters, Bellbirds, Tri-colored and Orange- fronted Chats, Red-cap Robins, Black-breasted and Spur-Winged Plovers, Little Bronze and Fan-tailed Cuckoos, Western Brown and Kestrel Hawks, Many-colored and Shell Parrots, Ring-necked Parrots, Welcome and White-backed Swallows, Wood Swallows, Rufus Song Larks, Harmonious Thrush, Bronze and Top-crested Pigeons, Tomtits, Short-billed Crows, Galahs, Cockatoos, and many others too numerous to particularise, as the auctioneer would say. Just prior to rough weather, Cranes, Seagulls, and Cormorants make their appearance. The sea shore, which is the natural habitat of some of these birds, is over 100 miles away. The ordinary Sparrow was reported to have reached Ooldea on its way West, but it was ruthlessly destroyed by the Inspector sent out specially for that purpose. Cockatoos and Major Mitchell Galahs congregate in great flocks at various times of the year, and their wild screeching echoes and re-echoes throughout the bush. On one occasion, many hundreds of cockies settled on the copper telegraph line at Ooldea, and gave a display of gymnastics on the unaccustomed wire, turning somersaults with the wire gripped in their beaks. Suddenly, amid the fearful screeching from the hundreds of birds, the line snapped and the cockies were forced to the wing. However, they immediately continued the performance on the second wire, but as another "fault" would have resulted, the cockies were dispersed and were kept so. Upon investigation, it was found that the sharp beaks of the birds had cut the wire as cleanly as if a knife or a file had been used, and the weight of so many of them on the span had caused the damaged wire to snap.

The Cave Owl of the Nullabor Plain. Remarkable for facial expressions.

Water-bearing Mallee. The Blacks obtain water from the roots of this tree.

5
THE VEGETATION OF THE WONDERLAND

One can find on some maps the words, "Ooldea Range," but one may search in vain for a line of mountains where the pine-clad ridges raise their torn and rugged battlements on high.

Instead, one would find row upon row of sand-ridges running north-west and stretching out into the Great Unknown. These sandhills are mysterious. They consist of a very fine, red sand, or rather a dust, and do net drift, but are covered with bushes, trees, spinifex, plants, etc., and if one were to dig down a few feet, one would find, most probably, a hard core of limestone. And in between the sand-ridges there are flats or valleys, with a generally hard surface, and containing clay pans, or small salt-beds, and supporting mulga and other valuable "top feed." Why these sand-ridges should run in a north-westerly direction, I cannot say, nor have I heard or read of any satisfactory explanation. Where the sand, or rather the dust, came from is another mystery, and the theory that it was blown off the Nullarbor Plain is a long way wide of the mark, inasmuch as similar sandhills are found hundreds of miles away from the Plain. How many ridges are there? Well, H.Y.L. Brown, the Government Geologist of South Australia, who made a geological exploration of this country in 1897, gives us the following typical entry in his diary: -

29th May. - Made a distance of sixteen miles over similar country to that traversed the previous day, crossing sixty-one sandridges, some of which were very steep and high. Quartzite and sandstone, with flint and jasper rock, outcropped in one of the flats between the ridges.

Now, as to the vegetation of this country. We find that the sandhills are covered with mulga, mallee, myall, myoporum, quondong, black oak, silky oak, native cork, acacia, spinifex, buck bush, saltbush, parakylia, bluebush, grass, etc. Almost all of these trees, bushes, grasses, and plants are edible by cattle, camels, sheep, and horses. Mulga is the favorite food of the camel, and cattle also are fond of it. It is an umbrella-shaped tree. Mulga country can be looked upon as very suitable for cattle and sheep.

Myall is a dark, dense, and heavy wood, with a smell of raspberry jam. The wood takes a beautiful polish, which brings out the lovely rich color. The finger-plates on the doors of some of the carriages on the Trans-Australian trains are made of this wood. It should be very suitable for "woods" (used in the game of bowls), but, unfortunately, it is very difficult to get timber that is free internally from cracks. This wood burns with a great heat, and leaves nothing else but a white ash. It is the principal firewood used in Port Augusta, and "along the line."

Mallee is of various kinds. One class of Mallee has large capsules of about two inches diameter, and bears a pink blossom, which is apparently full of honey, as in season it is alive with honey-making bees. Another class of Mallee is called "the water-tree," and is known to the blacks by the name of "Ngalda." This tree is easily distinguishable from the ordinary type by its brownish-tinged bark, the bark of the ordinary mallee having more of a whitish hue. From the roots of the brown-bark mallee, the blacks and the bushmen obtain water. The process is to cut a root into pieces and allow them to stand end up in a billy, a native utensil or weapon, or other receptacle, when the liquid will drain out. From a root one foot in length, one may obtain about eight ounces of water.

H.Y.L. Brown states in his diary that "it would be well if it were more generally known that good, fresh water can be procured from the roots of these mallees, and there is, therefore, no necessity for any traveller to go without water where they exist. The aboriginals depend upon these and a few other water-bearing trees almost entirely when they are travelling long distances from one rockhole or soakage to another."

The oaks (native name "Kooli") are also water-bearing trees, and the process of extracting water is similar to that of the mallee.

Where there are no mallees, oaks are found, and, of course, vice versa. When other sources of supply fail, the blacks turn to the trees, and of the two, the mallee is preferred. The roots of this tree radiate like a spider's legs, and consequently all the roots carry much more moisture than trees which have simply a main tap root.

Whilst on this matter, I may mention that when travelling the blacks secure water from certain hollow trees. These trees have hollow forks low down, and during the heavy thunderstorms which are experienced out here rain lodges in these cavities and remains there. The blacks know this, and they ascertain the location of the water by tapping with a stick. When they have located it, they obtain a good long spinifex stalk and pass it down into the water, which they then suck up through the hollow stalk. Of course, the quantity obtainable varies very considerably, according to the extent of the basin, in some cases only a single drink being procurable, in others quite a good supply. Mallees and oaks are the trees in which the hollows are generally found.

A yet further method of procuring water is for a black to draw upon an underground supply which is in the form of a long thin bulb growing on the roots of a particular species of grass. The blacks call it Joonga Joonga. It is a white bulb about two or three inches long, and very juicy. It is eaten either raw or roasted, and in each form it is by no means unpleasant to the taste. The tuber resembles a yam, but it is smaller, and obtainable in dry sandy areas.

The quondong, or native peach, flourishes in this country. These shapely trees have a foliage of a refreshing green, and when bearing fruit, they are very pretty.

The fruit consists of a large kernel, with a thin, edible covering. This fruit portion, when dried, is made into pies and jam, and is not by any means repellant.

Spinifex is of two kinds, one being edible by stock, and the other known as "porcupine grass," being of little value. The spinifex bears seeds on long thin stalks, and these stalks with the seeds are eaten by horses, cattle, and sheep. From the spinifex, the blacks extract a resin with which they attach the heads to the shafts of their spears.

Buckbush is regarded by some as a most nutritious food for sheep and cattle. When dry, the buckbush becomes detached from the ground, and it is then blown along by the wind.

As it travels along, it increases in size by the accession of other bits, until it is caught against a bush or fence. These then are the "Roly-polies" of the paddocks, and probably the nuclei of future sand-ridges, for the sand collects in the dried buckbush, and in the course of time it becomes a mound and eventually a sandridge.

The saltbushes (of which there are several kinds) are of the greatest statue as forage, especially in the remote interior, where they furnish a large bulk of succulent and nutritious food for sheep and cattle in the driest season of the year. Particular kinds supply a greater amount of fodder than others, or may be liked better by stock, but all of the saltbushes are valuable, with the exception, perhaps, of a few species that produce spines or thorns that injure the mouths or skins of animals, or burrs that might tend to deteriorate the value of the fleece. Saltbush is the great fodder of the low rainfall and hot country. The formation of its leaves is such that they have the power of retaining the dew that is precipitated during the nights in this country, and particularly on the Nullarbor. During railway construction days, "saltbush soup" was a favorite dish at some of the boarding-houses.

Bluebush is a small shrub that is found generally associated with saltbush, but not necessarily so. Portions of the Plain have bluebush, but no saltbush on them, and vice versa. As a fodder, bluebush is inferior to saltbush.

Perhaps the most wonderful plant in this district is the parakylia (or parachelia) which, for its nourishing value in periods of drought, is difficult to beat. Parakylia (*Calandrinia balonnensis*) is a member of the Portulaca family, and has a bright pink flower, which makes a fine show in its season. It has thick, juicy leaves, and therefore provides both food and water for stock. As one instance of its value as a fodder for cattle, I may quote the following case. Mr. A. H. Elliott, of Horseshoe Bend, Northern Territory, when giving evidence on oath before the Commonwealth Parliamentary Standing Committee of Public Works, stated:

If we get winter rain, we grow a herbage called parachelia, which, with an occasional shower, will last all the year. Horses will not live on it, but we have had cattle out in dry country for two years, and could not get to them; and when, after a shower of rain, we could get to them, we found them the primest cattle we have ever had. They had plenty of parachelia, and lived for two years practically without water.

I was out driving once at the back of the sandhills when the parakylia was in flower, and after arrival home I turned the pony out to forage for himself upon the saltbush, bluebush, spinifex and other edible scrub. I never worried if I did not see the pony for a day or two. It so happened that a long spell of dry weather ensued, and as the pony did not come in for a drink I became anxious about him. So I told Jimmy, one of the blacks, to find him, and bring him home, if alive. Jimmy set out on the track of the pony, and late that afternoon he returned to the camp and said to me, "I been seen 'em pony. Not your pony now, Missa Bolam! Him great big pfella!" and he demonstrated the size of the horse's girth by curving his arms in two huge arcs. The pony had returned to a patch of parakylia that he had noticed when we were out driving, and had been "in clover." This incident helps to dispel Mr. Elliott's idea, expressed in the previous paragraph, that "Horses will not live on it."

The Nullarbor Plain is, as its name implies, devoid of tree life, but whilst saltbush and bluebush form its chief vegetation, there are many other shrubs and grasses. Among the grasses may be mentioned wallaby grass, purple-topped grass, oat grass, spear grass, and Eragrostis lacunaria. All of these are excellent fodder, but with the spear grass when full grown, the awns or spears are injurious to stock and to the fleece of the sheep. In the depressions known as dongas, there is almost invariably a great profusion of grasses, buckbush, etc.

Blue-bush, the principal vegetation of the Nullabor.

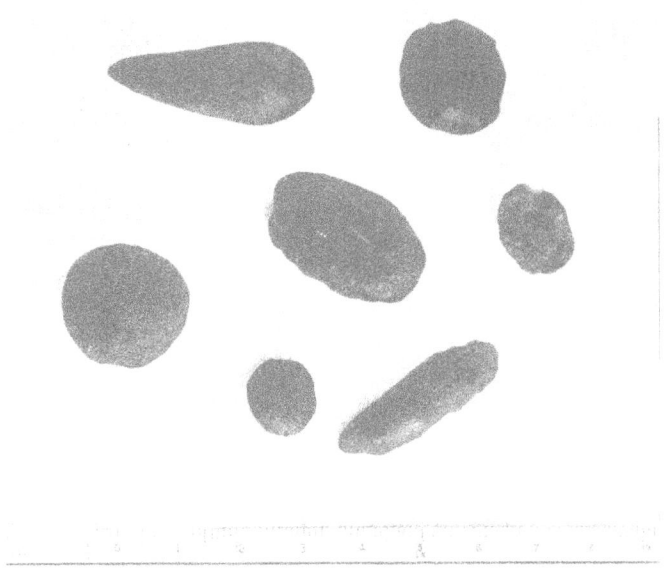

Australites - the Magic Stones of the Blacks, and the Mystery Stone of the Whites.

6

THE NULLABOR WONDERLAND

The mallee, the myall, the mulga, the myoporum, the oaks, the brooms, and other tree life peter out at Ooldea, and then there stretches out to the West, the North, and the South the Great Nullarbor Plain. For four hundred and fifty-seven miles the Trans-Australian Railway runs on the bosom of the plain in a direction that is almost due West; and it is across this stretch that the world's greatest length of absolutely straight line is to be found - a distance of three hundred and thirty miles. Standing on the line, one may look East and West, and see the shining bands of steel merge into each other - where the sky meets the land. Across this stretch of four hundred and fifty-seven miles of plain the land falls to the East at the average rate of nine inches per mile; so for all practical purposes one may say that the plain is almost dead level. How far to the North the plain extends is not definitely known, for no one has charted its limits. Giles, in 1875, must have been near its boundary, for he waits for a time in sandhill and spinifex country with salt lakes, marshes and mulga, mallee, casuarina, sandalwood and quondong; but after leaving Boundary Dam (which, by the way, was made by the blacks) he passed into grassy plains. In the previous year the Forrest brothers had crossed from Western Australia to South Australia, but they were 250 miles further North than Giles went in 1875, and were well North of the Nullarbor Plain. They went through the Musgrave Range, 280 miles North of Ooldea.

In 1857 two bushmen, Miller and Dutton, pushed out into the unknown land away to the north of Fowler's Bay. They came upon a treeless plain which stretched away as far as the eye could see. These were the first white men to see the Nullarbor Plain.

Delisser and Hardwike, in 1869, travelled from Fowler's Bay

into the plain in a north-westerly direction for about 240 miles, and reached scrub country just across the W.A. border. They described the plain as excellent pastoral country, if water could be obtained.

The southern limit of the plain is the limestone cliffs that overlook the Great Australian Bight, and they are from 60 to 200 miles away from the Trans-Australian Railway. From Twilight Cove almost to Israelite Bay, the cliffs rise vertically out of the sea to a height of 250 to 300 feet; but easterly from Twilight Cove they run back inland from the sea for some miles, and then trend roughly parallel to it as far as a point a few miles east of Eucla, where they again form the shore-line. The greatest distance of the cliffs from the ocean is at a point about half way between Eyre and Eucla, where they are some thirty miles inland; and this seems to indicate a comparatively recent uplift in this region.

The word "Nullarbor" is a combination of two Latin words, the adjective "Nulla," meaning "No," and the noun "Arbor," a tree. Thus the combined word, "Nulla-arbor," contracted to "Nullarbor," means "No-tree"; and a more appropriate name was never bestowed upon anything, for, with the exception of one comparatively small area, the Nullarbor Plain is as devoid of trees as the great ocean which it overlooks. It was Alfred Delisser who bestowed the name of "Nullarbor" upon this great Plain in 1866.

Aeons ago - perhaps a million years - what is now the Nullarbor Plain was the bed of an ocean; and a general and gradual uplift of the bed occurred until it reached its present height of about 800 feet above sea-level. In the faces of the cliffs at Twilight Cove, on the Great Australian Bight, and some distance back from the sea, and considerably above its present level, water-worn caverns and wave markings show that at one time the coast there the water supply gave out. It is quite likely, then, that further excavations in the sand and silt around all of these rocks would result in the discovery of the remains of more of these animals, and of others not dreamt of in our philosophy.

The whole area of the Nullarbor Plain is nearly a true level. Where it merges into the scrub country on either side, it is covered with a light red-colored loam, of varying depth; but that covering becomes thinner as one travels across, and one does not go far before flaggy limestone can be seen every here and there. Over the limestone country there is not even a thin thread of running water - in fact, this is so for the whole length of 1,051 miles of the Trans-Australian Railway - and the only surface water procurable is contained in small rockholes, which are few and far between, and, at the best, of a very limited capacity.

Studded all over the surface of the plain, and as far north as one hundred miles from the coast, are blow-holes, which are generally more or less circular pipe-like openings in the limestone crust, with a diameter of from one foot to eight feet. Through these openings the air often rushes with considerable force, and in some cases the outward draught is so powerful and constant as to keep a felt hat suspended in it. At other times there is a strong suction, and any light object held over the mouth of the blow-hole is drawn rapidly in. Some of the blow-holes are almost extinct, as far as their pneumatic action is concerned. The blow-holes prove the existence of caves, and the wide area over which the blow-holes are scattered leads one to believe that this wonderful plain will reveal caverns, the extent of which will exceed even the mammoth caves of Kentucky. Whether they will rival the beauties of Jenolan one dare not prophesy, and time alone can answer. But here is a field of exploration that calls loudly for the investigator; and he who hears and answers will be repaid with the wonders that await him in Subterrania. The blow-holes were undoubtedly rock-holes, and the water which collected therein gradually dissolved the limestone, and ate through to the caverns beneath, which were formed by water of unthinkable time before. Whilst the mouths of the blow-holes are of circular shape, the sides close in as they descend, and have ledges of rock, and the bottom is usually a crevice in the solid rock. The blow-hole in the morning may be issuing cool air, and in the evening it may be sucking it in. The air, as it is issued has a peculiar odor, somewhat resembling sea-weed. This fact has led some people to conclude that the issuing and sucking in of the air at the same blow-hole is due to tidal action at large caverns at the sea-front of the Great Australian Bight. Other investigators are decidedly of opinion that the outward and inward draughts are due to differences of temperature inside and outside the blow-hole. Some authorities maintain that the air rushing in and out of the blow-holes is accounted for by barometric pressure. If the blow-holes round about Ooldea were not so far from the ocean - a distance of 110 miles as the crow flies - one would incline to the first theory; but the cavern system is, in my opinion, so extensive that the compression due to tidal action would be exhausted in a few hundred yards. Here, then, is a field for the physicist to investigate, and its exploration may reveal some interesting and useful information. Arthur Mason, the Western Australian explorer, in 1896, had his camels stolen by the blacks when at Boundary Dam, and was compelled to walk 160 miles across the Nullarbor Plain to Eucla. Writing about the blow-holes, he says: -

After travelling about sixty miles, the extreme limit of the blow-holes was passed. Many were in full blast; in some the sound was like rushing water, in others like a train at full speed, and again like the noise of a hurricane. Many blow outwards, and others suck inwards. They are spirally formed, and are not more than eighteen inches to two feet in diameter. We found it very dangerous walking at night time, on account of the blow-holes, as they were hidden by the long grass. Being still on the plain, it was terribly cold at night, and there was no "wood to make a fire!" Mason was of opinion that the holes led to an immense quantity of water underground. H.C. Castilla, an engineer of the W.A. Public Works Department, who conducted boring operations on the Nullarbor Plain in 1902, stated: - "These plains, upland and lowland, are dotted with blow-holes. They are a very peculiar feature, acting as vents and drains. They emit a roaring noise, and blow in or out, according to the wind. After heavy rains I have seen considerable streams running into them. This explains why there is, despite a fair rainfall, little surface water or streams in the country."

I have been down several of these blowholes, and have entered many caves near the edge of the plain. The floor of each cave that I have been in contains masses of broken slabs of limestone. It is necessary to proceed very cautiously when in the caves, because frequently other holes are found in the floor and extending downwards. Where these holes lead to I cannot say, as, owing to the want of proper equipment, I have been unable to explore them, and no one else has tried. It is a pity that some adventurous spirit has not undertaken an exploration of these caverns, and revealed the wonders that lie there.

Wonders they will undoubtedly find; but you may rest assured that a complete survey of the caves of the Wonderland will be the work of probably a century, so extensive are they. In almost all the caves that I have been in, many cylindrical holes go upwards, but do not reach the surface, although in many cases only a foot of hard limestone separates the top from the surface of the land. It is evident that these holes were at one time blow-holes, but the water of ages left a deposit of lime in the mouth of the blow-hole, and this deposit grew, and eventually choked up the hole with a foot of cement.

Another peculiarity is that one blow-hole may have half-a-dozen or more openings to the outer air, at varying distances from each other. When driving in a buggy on the plain I have frequently noticed, a hollow sound as the horse's hoofs or the wheels of the buggy passed over the flat limestone. The hollow sound undoubtedly denotes the existence of a cavern immediately beneath the surface. The same hollow sound has been noticed by passengers, who get out at certain stations on the plain, and walk a short distance away from the line.

Every here and there on the Nullarbor Plain there exist shallow circular depressions in the surface, and these are called "dongas." The dongas vary in diameter from five chains to three miles, and the greatest have a depth of about 20 feet in the centre. They are undoubtedly formed by the caving in of subterranean chambers in the limestone. In the lowest part of the basin there is almost invariably a hole through which the water escapes. The dongas generally carry a good depth of soil, and grasses, buck-bush, etc., grow in great profusion in them. That beautiful flower, Sturt's Desert Pea, grows luxuriantly in all the dongas, giving a touch of vivid scarlet to the depressions. At a certain time of the year an exquisite perfume of clover floats from the dongas on a south-west breeze. A lovely, sweet, refreshing smell it is to us in the

A typical blow-hole, the Nullabor Plain is studded with them. They lead to caves.

A limestone curiosity; the "Billy Hughes" Rock.

sandhills, once experienced, ne'er to be forgotten; and when the bloom is no longer on the clover, then do we feel that something sweet has vanished temporarily from our lives, but it lingers in our memories until the day when spring again makes it a reality.

The great Nullarbor Plain, while devoid of trees, is covered with blue-bush, saltbush, cotton-bush, and other bushes, and in a good season a luxuriant growth of grass spreads over the land. In spring the everlasting daisies cover the ground, and from a distance one gets the impression of a snow-mantled area. But the stand-by of the plain is the saltbush, and the sight of it ever recalls to mind some lines from "Banjo " Paterson's 'In the Droving Days':-

"... And I crossed again
Over the miles of the saltbush plain -
The shining plain that is said to be
The dried-up bed of an inland sea,
Where the air, so dry and so clear and bright,
Refracts the sun with a wondrous light,
And out in the dim horizon makes
The deep blue gleam of the phantom lakes.
For those that love it, and understand,
The saltbush plain is a wonderland."

Animal life of various forms is to be found on the plain - kangaroos, dingoes, rabbits, bandicoots, small marsupials of different kinds, wild turkeys in hundreds, and other bird and reptile life. A remarkable feature is the immense number of very large dew shell-snails, which, in the early morning, or after a shower of rain, are seen traversing the ground in every direction.

7

THE GEOLOGY OF THE WONDERLAND

This is its poorest aspect; but what there is of it is of great interest. The Nullarbor Plain has already been dealt with in a special chapter; and our remarks will, therefore, be confined to the vicinity of Ooldea. Of gold, the metal of metals, there is no authentic trace. Prospectors penetrated into this region not many years after Giles, and then Tietkens, burst into the great unknown; and, like others in different parts, they claim to have discovered gold which never existed. The S.A. Government Geologist, after examining the country in 1897, reported that "the easy discovery of gold and other metallic minerals cannot be expected over the greater portion of the area traversed, owing to the prevailing covering of tertiary and secondary deposits and recent surface accumulations." The country, however, is rich in fossils embedded in the limestone. These fossils take the form of marine shells of various kinds, fish bones, corals, worms, etc. Marine shells in natural form have been found on the surface 40 miles north of the railway, or 140 north of the Bight. The bones of the great Diprotodon australis have been found on the Nullarbor Plain, and further discoveries of the remains of animals long since extinct are only a matter of time. Opals will also be found. Nodules of limestone, either loose or in conglomerate form, exist all over the country. Some of these assume curious shapes, resembling animals or other objects. In one case two large nodules were found attached, one being smaller than the other, and as the smaller one was on top it resembled a head on a torso. The head portion bore a likeness to a human face, certainly anything but handsome, and the railway construction men who found it therefore promptly named it "Billy Hughes," and as such it will go down to posterity.

Jasper, tourmalines and garnets are found, but the most unique stone occurring in this country is the mystery stone, which bears the name of skystone, australite, or obsidianite, and resembles the moldavite, billitonite and obsidian of other countries. Chemically, however, the sky-stones or australites are different from any terrestrial rock glasses (such as obsidian). These stones are jet black, hard enough to scratch glass, and generally of a roundish shape, the bottom half being globular, whilst the top is rougher, and has several indentations around it. They vary in size, some being only a quarter of an inch in diameter, whilst others are as much as, one inch. They can be cut into any desired form, and they polish beautifully. Some cut in diamond shape look very nice in brooches, rings, and so on when set in gold. The blacks call them "Nulu," and barter them with neighboring tribes as magic stones. They believe that the australite reached the earth from some extra-terrestrial region, and possess some magic power.

These "skystones" are found on various parts of the plain and among the sandhills of Ooldea. But what are they, and whence did they come? Various theories are advanced, those who favor a terrestrial origin stating that they are a volcanic product, or that they have been formed by lightning striking a whirlwind of sand. The first theory may be exploded by the fact that there is no trace of any volcano within five hundred miles or more from where the stones have been found; and the second theory seems to lose any weight it had when we say that the "skystones" are found well inland on the Nullarbor Plain, where whirlwinds of sand are unknown. The other body of theorists maintain that the stones come from the skies, and that they contain every indication of having been subjected to intense heat, and the indentations round the upper side are caused by friction during the passage through the air, whilst their occurrence on the plain away from every other rock but limestone can be accounted for in no other way. This is the general view, and it is the one to which we subscribe. Professor Howchin states that australites are now generally considered to be a peculiar form of meteorite which reached the Earth by means of a prehistoric meteor shower that covered a wide area, including a great portion of Australia.

The British Museum's authority, to whom specimens were submitted says: "They have not fallen from the stars, but are really a type of natural glass, found in several parts of the world. Their origin is not definitely known. They are known as australites, moldavites, and billitonites, and are closely related to basic or ultra-basic terrestrial igneous rocks." But then, of course, the same may be said of meteorites, inasmuch as they contain iron and other metals common to us.

Lignite or brown coal exists in large quantities in several places. At Pidinga, about 30 miles south of Ooldea, a bed of lignite occurs in a dry lake, and is traceable across the lake for a distance of about half a mile, which is the entire width of the lake, and down its course for a distance of a few miles. How much further it goes nobody knows. The bed of lignite is well defined and solid, and a trial bore put down proved that there was a body of coal 30 feet thick, then a stratum of grey clay and ironstone 9 feet in thickness, and more lignite, the depth of which is not known, as the bore went down only 40 feet. The structure and shape of the wood is visible in the upper portions of the bed, which also contains small pieces of fossil gum or resin. Samples of lignite which have been analysed give a generally large percentage of ash. Similar beds of lignite no doubt underlie parts of the Nullarbor and the sandhill country.

Whether oil is hidden in this Wonderland time alone will tell. A comparison of the strata of bores on the Nullarbor with those of the oilfields of Kansas shows a remarkable similarity of the material through which the bores passed. Large deposits of a bituminous material and another substance very much like parrafin have been found in the vicinity of White Wells, an out-station of Yalata, 60 miles south of the Trans-Australian Railway at Fisher.

Round about Ooldea one may obtain clays of various colors, some being pure white, others violet, yellow, brown, etc. These clays make fine models, which when baked in an oven become exceedingly hard. The white clays, of which there is an unlimited quantity, are probably suitable for fine pottery or china purposes. At any rate, they appear to me to be worth a trial.

Blacks from all parts with their spears. Mrs Daisy Bates in the centre. The fourth from right is holding a young dingo.

Wild Blacks just in from the Musgrave Ranges, an clothed by Mrs Daisy Bates.

8
THE WONDERLAND CLIMATE

Generally speaking the climate is hot in summer, and mild in winter. The average maximum temperature during the months of December, January, and February is 92.7 degrees, the average minimum 61.6 degrees, and the average mean 77 degrees; whilst in the winter months of June, July and August the figures are respectively 62.8, 38.8, and 51.2.

The climate of Ooldea and the Nullarbor is, in winter time, unsurpassed anywhere in Australia; that is to say, anywhere in the world. From a cloudless sky of Australian blue the sun shines down with a gentle warmth that is glorious to experience. A tinge of frostiness in the night and in the early morning sets the red corpuscles coursing rapidly through the veins, and for the rest of the day the body, absorbing the gentle rays, fairly glows with the comforting warmth. This is indeed the place: -

Where the air is clear as crystal, and the white stars fairly blaze
At midnight, in the cold   and frosty sky.

In the spring there is a coming warmth in the day, but the cold nights and the cool mornings are still with us. The shrubs and plants are in flower, and the birds are in the trees, making music all the day.

The summer days are hot, but the air is dry, and, although temperatures may be high, no great inconvenience is experienced. Despite the high temperatures that are occasionally met with we, our wives, and our little ones survive them all, and awake each morning as fit as a fiddle, after a refreshing sleep through the cool night. Each evening the sea breeze, originating in the Antarctic Ocean, sweeps across the plain - "O'er the sea bringing / Coolness to brow and breast
  Far away singing."

The autumn might well be called the spring, were it not for the falling leaves and the shortening days. And what of the rainfall? The following table tells the tale -

Rainfall in Points.

Month.	1917	1918	1919	1920	1921	1922
January	250	—	70	—	3	—
February	115	—	163	—	283	59
March	118	100	—	8	28	71
April	124	60	211	100	1	127
May	51	63	6	139	213	25
June	149	106	25	45	91	74
July	148	16	16	68	15	25
August	22	119	57	69	15	—
September	76	29	8	232	3	—
October	169	72	54	64	36	15
November	116	131	33	49	93	—
December	73	39	—	42	35	225
Total	1411	735	643	816	816	621
No. of Wet Days	15	30	27	47	43	34

The clearness of the atmosphere of the Wonderland is extraordinary, and has been often remarked upon by observers. The Carnegie Magnetic Survey was much impressed in 1912 by this feature, and its bearing on astronomy. The air seems to have a slight bluish tinge. The smoke of a train can be seen 45 miles away, and the shunting movements can be followed by means of the column of smoke. At night the headlight of an engine can be seen at least one and a half hours away, more particularly when the train is on the "straight" and coming East. In May, June, and July the visibility out on the Nullarbor is exceedingly pronounced, objects at a great distance being frequently seen. In the summer, however, the mirage appears soon after sunrise, and disturbs the definition. The mirage produces some remarkable effects.

Out on the Plain in the winter slight fogs occasionally occur in the early morning, and some beautiful fog rainbows are noticed. The warmth of the rising sun, however, soon dissipates the mists.

Owing to the radiation of heat being so rapid on the Nullarbor and the absence of clouds and other causes detrimental to the formation of dew, the air at night remains calm, saturation takes place quickly, and dew is precipitated. This occurs even in hot weather. The vegetation cools more quickly than the ground, and the leaves absorb moisture before dew is formed on the earth. Nature has provided the saltbush, bluebush, and other plant life out in this arid country with leaves that absorb dew quickly, and they thus get necessary moisture principally from the air, and not only from the ground. We are frequently asked how the animals in the Wonderland live, seeing that there is little rainfall and no surface water. Many of them suck the dew off the leaves of plants and bushes.

The Nullabor Plain and the world's greatest length of Straight line (330 miles).

9

THE ABORIGINALS

The natives seen at Ooldea offer a most interesting study, as Ooldea is one of the very few places in Australia where wild blacks from the innermost parts come into contact for the first time with civilisation. Blacks from the Mann Range, the Musgrave Range, the Everard Range, the Macdonnell Ranges, and other remote and unexplored regions of the interior, have, from time immemorial, come into Ooldea for the religious ceremonials, the corroborees, and to excl1ange articles for those made by their more "civilised" brethren. Many of these blacks - men, women and children - never saw a white man until they reached Ooldea; and, of course, on their arrival in camp they were dressed in nature's clothing. These wild blacks, therefore, afford an opportunity for study by the ethnologist, and which, if not seized, will soon vanish. I regret extremely to state that the black in this part of Australia is rapidly passing to his fathers. See these wild blacks as they come in from the ranges, in the pink of condition, after their trip of nearly 300 miles, their skins shining with the glow of health, their carriage graceful, their movements machine-like, and then see them, a month later, arrayed in the vilest of rags, themselves dirty, and their old-time customs being superseded by the traces of "civilisation," which they so readily acquire, and you see two different people. Captain Stokes, in his Discoveries in Australia, voices a fact, which other writers and observers corroborate. He says: -"I could not help comparing the bold, fearless manner in which they came towards us, their fine, manly bearing, head erect, no crouching or averting of eye, with the miserable objects I had seen at Sydney. I now beheld man in his wild state: and, reader, rest assured there is nothing can equal such a sight." When you observe these blacks at Ooldea begging "bacca" or a coin, I would implore of you not to imagine that they have always been so degraded-looking, but to reflect that you are viewing the victims of our flaunted civilization - blacks who are not black passing out of existence through contact with whites who are not white. These simple sons of the soil are regarded by many as the lowest type of mankind; someone has said so, and the hearers or the readers believe it. Let me say right here that the blacks are highly intelligent, and in many respects vastly superior to their white detractors. If their intelligence were of such a low order as their detractors would like us to believe, the blacks would be quite incapable of so readily copying the habits of the whites - even of enlisting, as many of them did, and fighting for freedom on the fields of France. They are wonderful men in the bush, living well in a country where whites would die in no time from thirst or hunger. The keenness of their eyesight and hearing is marvellous. Their knowledge of the habits of animals is astounding. The facility with which they acquire a working vocabulary of the English language is remarkable. Their power of endurance is extraordinary; their sense of honor is unimpeachable; whilst in proofs of loyalty they put many whites to shame. Just think of the wonderful devotion of Wylie, the black boy who accompanied Eyre in his mad march round the Great Australian Bight in 1840; of Charley, the native whose resourcefulness enabled Warburton to pull through in his journey from the north of South Australia to the north-west in 1873; of the great bushmanship of Jimmy, the old man, and of Tommy, the boy, who went with Giles in that daily duel with death in 1875; of those aboriginal members of Austin's exploring party in 1854, who, though themselves reduced to the utmost extremity by thirst, resigned to the lad Farmer (who had accidentally shot himself) their share of the water carried during two days; the kindness of the natives who gave fish and pidgery to Wills and King (of the Burke and Wills exploration) in 1861, and showed them how to make bread from nardoo, and their subsequent kindness to King; the marvellous resource-

The women of Ooldea, 1920.

A group of families surround Daisy Bates.

fulness of Windich, one of the two blacks who accompanied John and Alexander Forrest in their journey from Champion Bay to the overland telegraph line, and thence to Adelaide, in 1874; the wonderful devotion of Jacky Jacky, who accompanied Kennedy on the ill-fated expedition to the Cape York Peninsula in 1878; of the skilful hunting ability of the two blacks, Charley and Harry Brown, who went with Leichhardt to the Gulf of Carpentaria, and on to the Port Essington settlement in 1845. And so one may go on examining the diaries of the heroic explorers, and one finds the same feature in each - a plain, unvarnished tale of unstinted praise for the black members of the expeditions. But let us pass over in silence the awful atrocities which other men, called explorers - McKinlay, for instance - perpetrated upon these black boys of the bush: and of those whites who shot blacks "just for practice," etc. Thank God those dark days are over, and civilisation reached the blacks at Ooldea in a more enlightened age!

OOLDEA TRIBE. - It is a matter of the greatest regret for me to record that not a single black of the original Ooldea tribe is now alive. The Ooldea blacks were known as the Koogurda, or meat-eating tribe. Of course, there are many blacks frequenting the district, but they consist of members of all the surrounding tribes. Many of these blacks, having once tasted the white man's food, will not go back to their old grounds, and so the existing tribe remains at about the same numerical strength, the new arrivals from the Musgrave Ranges (280 miles to the north) filling up the gaps caused by those who pass over "the Great Divide." On very many occasions blacks, who have never seen a white man, come down from the ranges in the north. They arrive, of course, in the nude, but are soon made presentable by the other natives. These ranges are estimated to be distant from Ooldea as follow: - Macdonnell, 470 miles; Musgrave, 280 miles; Everard, 235 miles. And during the long trip down the blacks live by obtaining water from their "native wells" and from the roots of trees, and their condition on arrival is wonderfully bright and clean. When they put on clothes, however, they become subject to colds, which lead to running noses; and, as the blacks do not wash themselves, they soon get into a dirty state, which is not helped at all by the filthy cast-off clothing which they wear. In this case, the old saying of "Clothes make the man" is given the lie. The blacks thus equipped would not do credit to a "Pelaco" advertisement; but in their wild state Web Gilbert could well take some of them as physical models of graceful carriage.

SOCIAL LIFE. - The blacks are nomads, that is to say, they have no fixed abode, but wander over the country, either as the whim takes them, or in accordance with some pre-arranged plan. In days long gone by their wanderings were probably restricted to tribal boundaries. The longest they remain in one locality is generally a week, and then off they go to a new camp, which may be only a few hundred yards away from the former spot. The reason for this change of home may be due to the necessity of food supplies, the death of one of the tribe, sanitation, the proximity of wood, and so on. Deserted camps are thus scattered all over the countryside. Being wanderers, their "homes" are of the most primitive construction. They are known as "wurleys," and are constructed of parts of branches of trees placed in the ground, and arched over at the top, so as to give support to one another; and the structure is, with the exception of a small opening for entrance and exit purposes, then covered with bags, brush, or other available material. The "doorway" is located according to prevailing weather conditions, and, as the wind changes, so the openings are shifted. The wurleys vary in size, an average being about eight feet in diameter, and about six feet in height. A fire is usually lighted right at the "doorway," and during the night it is kept constantly going, for the nights in this country are, even in summer, cool, if not positively cold. In winter fires are even lighted right inside the wurley; and frequently there will be two fires inside, about a yard apart, the occupants sleeping in between them. In the restlessness resulting from dreams the black rolls on to the fire; and I have frequently seen on their bodies scars caused by fire burns. Looking from a distance across at the blacks' camp in winter time one gets the impression of the lights of a small city, from the many little spots of twinkling fire seen in all directions. Another practice of the blacks is to light a fire upon some sand, and, when the fire has been going suffiently long to warm the sand beneath it, the ashes are scraped away. The heated sand on the surface is also scraped away until quite a cavity is formed. In this depression the black will lie down, and the warmth of the sand serves as a heated bed. Many of the blacks have very scarred backs, and in very many cases the scars have been caused by lying in the cavity too soon after the fire has been removed, and getting burnt by so doing.

FOOD. - In pre-railway days, and also to-day in the back country, the food of the blacks was whatever they could obtain by hunting, by strategy, or as a gift from nature. It consisted of lizards, snakes, grubs, bardies, kangaroos, dingoes, rabbits, bustards, mallee fowls, other birds, eggs, fruit from native trees, etc. To-day those along the railway line live on the food they can get from the trains, and whatever is given to them by the whites; but, in justice to the blacks, it should be said that they also purchase food with the money they procure from the sale of boomerangs, etc., to passengers, and from dingo scalps and skins. The blacks imitate the whites, even to the extent of preferring the food of the whites to what they can themselves obtain.

Their cooking methods are very primitive. When an animal is caught, the black usually disembowels it, and then places it into a heap of ashes. It is a common thing to see a dozen or more rabbits being cooked in the one fire. The animal is not skinned, but the "innards" are simply removed, and the carcase is cooked. A hole is excavated in the sand, hot ashes are placed therein, the bodies of the animals are placed on top of the ashes, and more ashes are placed over all, completely covering the whole lot up. Birds are cooked in somewhat similar fashion to animals, excepting that they are not disembowelled, but placed straight on the ashes, as described above. This method of cooking may not please M. Soyer, but, from the point of view of the black, it is just "it" if the fur or feathers are burnt off. Thus it is not by any means an uncommon thing to see a red streak down each side of a black's whiskers during or shortly after his dining upon one of these delicacies. Whenever large game is caught, it is not brought back to camp, but a fire is built at the site of the kill, and there the hunters will remain until all is devoured.

The black has a peculiar way of eating an egg. It is usual for him to prick each end, and allow the white of the egg to run away; and he then eats the yolk. He invariably does this with the eggs of the mallee hen. If, when pricking the egg, it is found that a chicken is inside, the value of the delicacy is greatly enhanced, and the luxury is entirely consumed.

DEATHS. - The blacks ordinarily regard a death as a very important matter, and news of it is sent to various places where blacks are camped. A young girl died recently down at the Coast, and a messenger was despatched all the way to Ooldea - about 120 miles - to report the event. Messengers are sent out to carry the news of almost every occurrence of an important nature. I ascertained this fact in a curious way. Some black children asked me to show them a book of photos., which I did; and they proceeded to name the different people the photos. represented. I noticed that they omitted repeatedly to name a photo. of a little black girl; and as I knew that the girl and they had been playmates, I said, "That one Arlie!" Turning to me, they said very softly, "Arlie all finish up." Scarcely able to believe it, as I had seen Arlie only a few months previously, I said, "All same Jimmy?" who had died recently at Ooldea. "Oo-ah! (yes!)" they whispered. "Who told you?" I asked; and one of the boys replied, "Sonny bring news up from Coast." I recollected Sonny arriving by himself a few months back; and it was now clear to me that he had been a messenger sent with the news of Arlie's death.

The blacks avoid mentioning the name of any deceased person, and they refrain from looking at a photo. of him or her. One day when looking through a copy of *The Trans-Australian Wonderland*, some of my black friends came across the photo. of Jimmy (Jagella), who died a few months after it was taken, and they immediately closed the book; and when I asked them the reason why, they would not reply.

BURIALS. - Dr. Albert Churchward, in his *Origin and Evolution of Primitive Man*, describes the Australian aboriginal as belonging to the Heidelberg or Neanderthal group, and, in support of this statement, he quotes the way in which the body is prepared for burial, viz., the thrice- bent position. This is most interesting, as some of the blacks are to-day buried in this thrice-bent posture. Generally speaking, a black will not allow a white person to be present at a burial, but occasionally, in the case of a favored person, this prohibition is not strictly enforced. Once I was privileged to be present at the burial of a child. The body had been bound up so that the elbows rested on the chest, and the hands covered the face, whilst the legs were doubled so that the knees almost touched the elbows. A grave had been previously dug, about three feet deep, in a sandy slope, and in a north-south direction, and in this grave some green bushes had been placed. Upon these bushes the body, wrapped in the apparel which had been worn by the child, was deposited on its side, with the head pointing northwards. Some more bushes were then placed on the corpse, until they were up to ground level. Over these bushes logs were placed crosswise, together with bark, and the whole was finally covered with sand. Whilst the last bushes were being placed on the corpse, one of the blacks delivered a speech, apparently to the body before him, as his eyes never left the grave. When the last of the sand was thrown over, the blacks moved away without making the slightest sound. The last act in the burial was the lighting of a good-sized log at one end, which would probably keep burning for some days. Whilst the burial was in progress, there was a general silence, but no sooner had the mourners returned to camp than they broke out into an almost indescribable wailing. After this crying, the whole camp was shifted, and at dusk another wailing was set up, which continued far into the night. Whenever another black arrived at the camp the whole process of wailing would be renewed, no matter how long it might be after the burial.

The grave will not be visited again, and the locality even will be avoided for many months; for the blacks think that the spirit of the departed one will haunt the place for a long, long time, and will wreak vengeance upon any intruder upon his solitude.

When Jimmy (Jagella), a young man of the Dingo totem, died recently, and was buried, I carefully noted the circumstances attending the burial. The grave is situated on the northern slope of a sandhill, about 200 yards away from where he died. It is approximately five feet deep, 36 inches long by 22 inches wide, with rounded ends. The ground had been cleared for about 15 yards all around, the brush being used for purposes of the grave. The sand had been thrown out on the west side, and left in a heap at the head of the grave, which faces East and West. The interior of the grave was all brush; the body was laid upon a foot of brush, and brush was placed on top of the body and packed tightly right up to the surface. Small logs were then placed lengthwise over the grave, and then on top of the logs more brush was placed, and finely ovalled off. No sand or earth whatever was placed in the grave, and no sand covered the body. The usual method of tying the knees to the thighs, and tying the arms together (thus placing the body in the thrice bent position), had been followed, and the head faced the West. Both men and women took part. in the burial service, the women walking on each side of the body with lighted torches. At the graveside the body was lowered to two relatives standing in the grave, and they placed it in position, and stacked the brush around it. After the burial, fires were lit in several places-East, North, and West- but there was no fire on the Southern side of the grave, where the black died. There is no doubt also that the camp was left very hurriedly, for clothing, hats, and cooking utensils were scattered about.

CLOTHING. - As far as clothing is concerned, the blacks have, in their wild state, none at all; but, when in touch with civilisation, old clothes are eagerly sought after, and they are always worn in the presence of the Whites. These old clothes are worn until they are almost in shreds, but, nevertheless, be it said to their credit, the blacks will not venture near the siding without these rags hanging on them. In the camp life clothes are dispensed with a good deal, but should the blacks see a white coming to the camp, a general rush would be made for their clothes.

SANDALS. - The blacks are very fond of dogs, and no camp is complete unless a lot of curs are hanging about. Dingo pups are obtained about August, and, to get them, the blacks have to go out into the porcupine-grass country. For these trips a kind of sandal, or covering for the foot, is made from rabbit-skin. This skin is pulled over the foot when in a green state, and the neck part of the skin is tied at the toe, and the skin is brought round the ankle from the back by means of the two back legs, skinned out, and the two legs are then tied in front. In the case of a sore foot or an injury to it, a rabbit skin is tied over the injured part, and this acts as a bandage.

NO AUTHORITY.- It may be said that the blacks have no permanent hereditary chiefs. There are men among them who, by the weight of their arm or their great fighting ability, have won a kind of temporary power, and there are in the tribesmen of superior intellect; but there is no evidence that they hold any prescribed authority over the actions of others, excepting by a tacit understanding. The absence of authority is strikingly manifested in the camp life, where small groups often fight among themselves, and there is nobody who has authority to quell the disturbance. I shall quote a few cases in support of this statement. One night, at Ooldea, a great howling and crying was heard over at the blacks' camp, and, on investigation as to the cause, it was ascertained that a few months previously a nunga had stolen another black's lubra, and, on his return to Ooldea, he was met by her rightful lord and master. A quarrel immediately arose, and it resulted in the rightful hubby giving No. 2 and the erring lubra a sound hiding. Before long, however, the defeated Lothario collected his friends, and a free fight followed, which might have ended very seriously if the police had not intervened. There was no person among the blacks who had the authority of a policeman. On another occasion two young boys began a fight, and, when their respective parents appeared, they bandied out a few words, which resulted in their having a set-to. An onlooker, seeing one of his friends getting the worse of the scrap, joined in, and that brought a supporter of the other side into action, and the general melee resulted in one of the blacks being speared. There being no authority vested in any one of the blacks, a white man intervened and stopped the conflict. In describing the fight, the winner said: "He get hit across 'em back of neck; lose 'em thinkem and go mad; kill 'em one, but not finish 'em all up; then spear 'em other."

BARTERING. – The blacks, like other primitive people (and not unlike some white races to-day), traded by bartering. Their economic system had not developed to the extent of employing a medium of exchange. But at Ooldea, and at other places where they touch the line, they rapidly acquire the money-making habit, and they quickly recognise and appreciate coins of various values. By the process of bartering, the products of the north of Australia find their way to the Great Australian Bight, and those of the west to the tribes in the east. Thus it is a common thing to find a pearl shell from the north of Australia tied around the neck of a black who has come into Ooldea. Pearl shells have a great fascination for most blacks. One day a black at Ooldea was exhibiting a "pretty stone," which was embedded in his wommerah, or spear-thrower, and quite a sensation was caused when it was seen to be a nugget of gold. The whites who saw it thought they were on the track of another Golden Mile, and, with the object of ascertaining the whereabouts of tlle hidden treasure, the black was closely questioned, but answered "Mucka-mel" The following conversation took place (the words in parenthesis being my translations) :-

White: "Balya one!" (Good one!)
Black: "Oo-ah l" (Yes!)
White : "Me want coog-ha !" (I want one.)
Black: "Mucka-me, only coog-ha!" (No, only one!)
White: "Waijela bool-ga munda ?" (White fellow dig big earth?)
Black : "Weir! An-gool-a-jing wongi bool-ga woomerah!" (No! When I was going about I had a big talk with a fellow, and gave him a woomerah for it!)
White: "Oh, I see; wongi, and give wommerah for pretty stone!"
Black : "Oo-ah!" (Yes.)

The black had bartered his woomerah for the nugget of gold, probably with a black of a Western Australian tribe, from perhaps Kalgoorlie, Laverton, or some other auriferous field. Thus, articles which are plentiful in one black's country are bartered for those which are rare in his, but common in some other part.

SMOKING. - Unfortunately the blacks copy the whites in some comparatively useless habits, of which smoking is the principal. Perhaps the cause of this is the fact that generally the first whites they come in contact with are smokers. The habit of smoking is so deeply rooted in the blacks that it is usual for even very small child ren to beg for "bacca," and it is no uncommon sight to see a child sucking its mother's pipe while sitting on her lap. The older blacks, men and women, are fond of chewing tobacco - the darker the better. After a good chew, the wad is taken from the mouth and placed away for further use, and this procedure is repeated until the wad is completely exhausted. Drinking likewise would be freely indulged in if the law did not prohibit it. They quickly see the advantage of the white man's ways of doing things, and thus we find that the nullah, the sling and the spear are readily laid aside for the gun and the rifle.

MARRIAGE. - The marriage system of the blacks is, in the opinion of white investigators, very complicated at first sight; but when the full meaning of their social basis is grasped we find that the system is simple. In the first place the black calls all of his father's brothers (i.e. paternal uncles, according to our system) "Father"; and, secondly, he calls all of his mother's sisters (i.e. maternal aunts in our case) "Mother." According to the laws of the blacks a marriage cannot therefore take place between their father's brother's son or daughter and their mother's sister's son or daughter. They are regarded, according to tribal custom, as of close blood relationship. Marriage can, however, take place between a black's mother's brother's children and his father's sister's children. Therein lies, generally speaking, the fundamental principle of the whole of their marriage system. There may be very slight variations from the above in certain localities, but the system described appears to be the common basis. But when the white man came to these parts the rigidity of the black's marriage laws began to relax; and as civilisation means that a man cannot take the law into his own hands and inflict a penalty, the young blacks, observing this protection, and being copiers of the whites, break away from the former sacred customs, and the power of the old men of the tribe to impose the death penalty on an offender no longer exists. The old men lose control of the tribe, and once that control vanishes it cannot be regained so long as the blacks keep in touch with civilisation. Their children, reared at the railway camps, adopt the practices of the whites, and become careless of their own; or perhaps they do not even know the native customs, for as the old man drops out there go with him many of the carefully guarded secrets of his tribe. A nunga is not necessarily restricted to one wife; he may have three or four.

NAMES OF OFFSPRING. - Babies of either sex take the name or totem of the country ill which they were born, irrespective of the totem or country to which their parents belong. For instance, an Allen-jurra man (Northern area) marries a Will-yarra woman (Western area), and they eventually reach the coastal area of Fowler's Bay, where a child is born. This child, by that fact, becomes a Coastal countryman, or takes the particular totem of the area in which it is born. Later on the married couple arrive at Ooldea, where another child is born. This child belongs to the Ooldea area.

WEAPONS. – The blacks never had a big variety of weapons, and those used to-day are probably of the same kind as their ancestors employed right back in the haze of antiquity. The principal weapons of offence and defence are the boomerang, the spear, the waddy (nullah), the wommerah (or spear-thrower) and the shield. The advent of civilisation has caused improvements in the methods of manufacture, and in some cases in the materials used for the spear heads. Thus the tomahawk and the knife would be used in making boomerangs, etc., instead of the flint, and spear heads would be made from glass and porcelain (from the insulators on the telegraph lines), instead of from stone. Of the weapons of offence the boomerang holds pride of place, and it is practically in everyday use. There are two distinct kinds of boom-

A passing water expedition through Ooldea Station in 1920.

Children play around Ooldea Station in 1920.

rangs, viz., the one which is thrown, and returns on its own axis to the thrower's feet, and the other, which is thrown straight ahead, and does not return. This fact is not generally known to the traveller on the "Trans.," and, consequently, many amusing instances have been noticed of a passenger throwing a boomerang which he expected would return, but which sailed right ahead, and thus necessitating the thrower chasing it. On his return after recovering the weapon, the passenger, if not a "sport," might accuse the black of selling him an inferior boomerang, little thinking that his own knowledge was at fault at not being able to differentiate between the boomerang employed in hunting and that used for amusement. The returning boomerang is thrown in one of two ways - it may be thrown in the air at an angle of 45 degrees with the ground, or it may be thrown so that it will strike the earth about 25 yards away with a gradual downward tendency, and, after hitting the ground, it will rise suddenly to a great height, the while performing graceful gyrations, such as a boomerang only can go. These boomerangs are, of course, always thrown in the wind to obtain the best display. The non-returning boomerang is used in hunting and in fights. An object on the ground - say, a sitting rabbit - is the target, and the boomerang is thrown at it. When it hits the ground, it rises slightly, but the gyratory motion and the shape of the weapon brings it to earth again, and that continues until the force is spent. Anything in the line of flight gets hit, and hurt. I have seen one of these boomerangs thrown a distance of 175 yards, without taking into account the ricochets. It is highly dangerous for a careless spectator to get in the line of fire of a boomerang thrower. It is likewise dangerous (and expensive) for an interested passenger to experiment in boomerang- throwing close to the train. Many a window has been broken in this way; and, whilst the blacks at Ooldea are very careful to avoid any occurrence of this nature, it has been found necessary to request that the throwing of boonlerangs be conducted a little distance from the train whilst it is standing at Ooldea. When you are buying a boomerang from a black at Ooldea, remember that you are not necessarily getting a man-killing instrument, but rather a "blackfellow's plaything." You will, however, be buying a genuine boomerang, made by the blacks with infinite labor, and well worth the "bob" or two that the native asks for it. Treat these blacks, then, a little generously, and their happy smiles will be something given in with the unique boomerang, which you should be proud to possess.

For the making of a boomerang a branch with the necessary bend is selected. After being chopped out from the tree the boomerang-to-be is roughly trimmed with the useful tomahawk, then chiselled to proper shape with glass, and afterwards smoothed with sand or glass, the final decorations being made with a pen-nib fixed in a wommerah. The wood used is principally mulga or needlewood. During the preparations for the ceremony in honor of H.R.H. the Prince of Wales, some of the blacks were driven about the bush for the purpose of sighting suitable bends from which to make boomerangs, and which were then, of course, secured. The blacks have frequently told me that all suitable bends have been cut out in this district; and this fact is quite understandable when one reflects that the passengers buy numbers from the natives, and the demand is greater than the district is capable of supplying.

The spears are used in hunting and in fighting, and, when thrown by means of the wommerah, they are hurled with great force, and for a considerable distance or height, and, needless to say, with almost uncanny accuracy - an art acquired by long years of experience. These spears may be of local manufacture by the blacks, or they may have been acquired in the process of bartering. They are generally made from long, thin mallee shoots. Bends are taken out by holding the crooked part in hot ashes built up into a small mound, and, when hot, by pressing each side of the bend down until straightness is obtained. All former bends are carefully gone over again, and the finished stick is turned out very straight. Glass is used for trimming, or, if obtainable, rasps and files for the rough work and broken glass for trimming. The smaller end has a little round hole made in it, so that it will fit the wommerah. The spear head varies according to the purpose for which it is intended. Generally, however, there is a sharpened piece of wood bound on to the spear in a slanting position, so that when the spear goes through the object it cannot be pulled out the way it went in. For rabbiting and such like a spear with a plain sharpened point is used.

I went out one day to watch a black friend make a shield. After selecting a suitable tree (an oak), my friend commenced operations. In place of the old stone implement he unhitched a small sharp tomahawk from his belt. Large cuts were made top and bottom about two feet apart, a line was cut down each side, and with a flat piece of wood he prized the future shield from the trunk of the tree. The piece was thoroughly straight-grained, without a flaw, with the nice rounded surface of the tree trunk. The tomahawk was again used very accurately, and much of the inside was chipped away, leaving a large portion in the centre for the armpiece to be eventually made from. The inside was then cut away by tomahawk and stone axe to the same shape as the outside. In chipping, the wood is stood up on end, the bottom resting on the work-man's foot, who is, of course, squatting on the ground. His heel serves as the block. Once when the tomahawk slipped and fell with force on his heel I held my breath; but no harm resulted - the axe simply bounced off. The black certainly took no notice. The inside of the shield was then smoothed with bits of glass, the outside with sand or glass. When completed, decorations are made with a pen-nib gummed on to the end of the wommerah. Finally the whole is rubbed over with red clay mixed with oil or fat.

TOOLS. - The blacks are the last of the Stone Age Men; but they are rapidly passing to the Steel Age, an evolution which is occurring more quickly in their case than in that of any other people. Yet, some stone implements are still in use, and will probably survive. There are three, viz., the sacred initiation stone, chippings for toolmaking, and the grinding stone. It is well for the reader to remember that Ooldea is situated in the sand ridge country, and, consequently, there is no suitable stone here for implement making, nor has there ever been. The original Ooldea blacks were therefore, not perfect stone implement makers. Stones have been brought here by blacks from other parts who have made implements out of them, or they have reached here through the barter routes of distant days. I have never seen old axe heads, stone spear heads, or stone knives in the possession of local blacks. If they ever did have any, the implements vanished long ago.

Initiation stones are traded articles, as there are no suitable stones for the purpose in this locality. They are small flints with a knife edge, and are carefully preserved in wrappings (generally of skin), and are treasured with the greatest care. In fact, if you were fortunate enough to have the opportunity of seeing one, you would be surprised at the length of time it takes the black to unwrap the covering. Very rarely will a black consent to any white man seeing the stone, and never a female, for if one were to see the magic stone it would probably result in the death of the woman.

There are two grinding stones, the bottom one being flat, although there may be grooves in it caused by the operation of the top stone; and the top one, which works in the grooves of the bottom one, is rounded. In between these stones native seeds are ground to a flour, which before the advent of the white man was much in use; but now wheaten flour has almost eliminated the need for grinding stones, and, consequently, they are being discarded. There are very few about here now, for they have either passed into the hands of collectors for museums, etc., or have been covered over by the sand drifts. Inland and away from access to the white man's flour the grinding stones are, of course, still in use.

Small chippings in thousands are to be found out at the Ooldea Soak. Some are lying on the surface, others are buried deep in the sand, and each wind that blows either uncovers or covers hundreds of others. The chippings (it may be more correct to call them knives) are made from a selected stone. This stone is usually chosen with great care, for much depends on a straight, clean chip. Hammer stones are made by knocking all the protruding edges off, leaving the stone with a rough, circular appearance. These hammer stones vary considerably probably on account of the class of chipping required. For general use one with a diameter of about one and a half inches meets the case. The hammer stone is held in the hand, and with a slanting downward movement it strikes the edge of the stone held in the other hand, and from which the intended chip is to be taken. Considerable skill is necessary in order to obtain a fine clean chip. Sometimes the chip thus obtained is suitable without further work on it, but if not it is very gently chipped with a smaller hammer stone until a fine edge is obtained. When the chipping is complete it is gummed on the end of a wommerah. The method of gumming is very simple. A hard black mass of gum obtained from the porcupine grass is slowly heated over a fire until it is quite pliable. It is then worked up in the hands, and when at the right consistency it is placed all around the stone and its backing of wood. When set the gum is remarkably solid, and will stand a great amount of usage. Where a very strong implement is wanted the stone is bound on with a piece of sinew, and then over all the gum is placed. With the sharp edge of the stone outward and the back gummed to the wommerah, the implement is complete, and takes the place of a chisel with the black. (Pen-nibs are also placed in the end of a wommerah in like manner, excepting that the pointed end is gummed on, and the rounded end, which has been sharpened, is used.)

NATIVE STRING. - String making or spinning from hair or from the fur of animals is a universal avocation of all blacks, even children being sometimes so engaged. Whilst the local blacks have apparently never been able to make ornamentations (which come down through the barter routes from Northern Australia), they can and do make string, which they put to a great variety of uses, but principally as bands for the hair, decorations, the strings of weapons, etc. Their method of making string is simple, but tedious. Two small sticks about four inches long are obtained, and one is placed across the other in the form of a cross. This is used as a winder, and this and a bundle of wool, hair, or fur are all that is required. The black sits down, and the wool, hair, or fur is thinned out with the hands, and then rubbed vigorously up and down upon the naked thigh, until the desired thickness is obtained. As the thread or string is made, it is wound across the winder for future use. Wombat's fur is used chiefly for pads for the head. White fur from the tails of rabbits is woven into forehead hands. Human hair is frequently cut and made in to string, which is used on sacred weapons, or as neck hands. Wool is now greatly in demand in place of native string, and old socks and other articles are always unthreaded for the wool.

WHIP-MAKING. - Crack! Crack! Crack! Looking out of the window I saw a black boy cracking a whip. "Where you get that whip, eh?" I asked. "Make 'em," was the reply. "Show me. Freddie." And a whip about the size of an ordinary buggy whip was handed to me. On examining it I saw that the handle was a piece of mallee, barked and of a whitish color. The lash was a strip of mallee bark tapered. One end was bound round the handle in such a fashion that it could not slip, and the other end was unwoven in such a manner that it looked like a bunch of cotton thread. It was this last portion that made the "crack!" "What you use this one for?" I queried. "Only play 'em!" came the reply. "Sometimes make 'em mulga, sometimes make 'em mallee: all same whip."

WATER CARRYING. - The blacks are adepts at balancing articles on their heads. They use kerosene tins for carrying water to the camp; but the tin is never carried by hand, as is the custom of the whites, but is placed upon the head and carried away. Their skill in balancing and carrying heavy articles on the head is remarkable. For this work they use a kind of circular pad of string, which they make from the fur of wombats and other animals. The pad is really a circular ring from one to two inches thick, and is placed upon the head. On this the kerosene tin is placed, whilst the carrier is in a sitting position, and the black then rises and marches off. The lubras generally do the carrying, and one frequently sees a woman with a full kerosene tin on her head, and a billy can in each hand. A peculiar custom of theirs is to place a few small bushes on the top of the water. This prevents the water from spilling, besides forming a rest for flies and such like. To watch a gin carrying a tin on her head, lowering and rising with it, makes one expect to see it fail; but I have never known such a thing to occur.

FIRE-MAKING. - Before the coming of the white man the blacks used their own methods of fire-making, and as these, like many other native practices, are being abandoned for the easier ways of the whites, it is fitting that I should place on record how the blacks made their fires, and the means which are still pursued in those remote parts of the interior where the convenient match is not available. The blacks have three or four ways of fire-making, but the one I am now about to describe is the method in general use in this locality. Probably it has been handed down through the ages with slight modifications as better tinder became available. It is an easy means of producing a flame, and a knowledge of the method should be of value to any person who may be so unfortunate as to be 100 miles from home with the last match dead in his hand. The materials required are a fairly large piece of very dry wood (quondong is preferred here) with a crack in one side, a smaller piece of hard wood with a sharpened edge, some rabbit manure, some fine grass and sticks. With these materials at hand the black sits down with the large piece of wood in front of him, crack uppermost. The fine grass is placed in the crack to make a fairly firm bottom, then powdered rabbit's manure is dropped in to about a quarter inch from the top and patted down. The sharp edge of the small piece of wood is now drawn backwards and forwards across the crack over the rabbit manure, slowly at first, but more vigorously as the smoke appears. The working of the stick makes a groove in the other wood, and each side of the crack is now filled with the powdered wood resulting from the operation. The rabbit manure commences to smoke, and is gently raised with a stick, and more powdered manure is dropped on it. The grass and leaves are made into a heap with powdered rabbit dung in the centre, and the smoking manure from the crack in the wood is turned into the grass held in the hand This is now gently rolled up and lightly blown at. Smoke then arises, and the grass bursts into flame. The manure which was smouldering in the crack comes out in one piece, as the particles of powder adhere together through the heat generating.

A more modern method is to use newspaper instead of grass. The blacks soon learnt that newspaper was easier than grass to ignite, and this is another proof of their aptitude to learn. In the method described above it is necessary to have very dry wood and a sharp razor-blade stick with a fairly wide back, so that a little pressure can be placed upon it when rubbing.

Another instance of the adaptability of the black is the use of a piece of mirror or any magnifying glass for fire-making. Whilst I was over near the camp to-day a black asked me for the loan of the portrait attachment off my camera lens. I complied with his request. "That one balya (good)!" he said, as he made a little hole in the sand, into which he put some powdered rabbit dung, then holding the portrait attachment in a slanting position and as steady as a rock for a few minutes, he produced first smoke, then flame. A looking-glass answers the same purpose. So when you give a black a looking-glass you please him immensely, for he loves to slip away to a quiet corner to admire his own grim beauty and stir up the flames of love, whilst he has also at hand a ready means of producing a flame of more practical use.

SMOKE SIGNALS. - As is known to all travellers in the territory of the blacks, the latter are able to communicate with each other over considerable distances by means of smoke signals. It is incredible to white people how the blacks can read the messages conveyed by the smoke, but that they do read them is indisputable. I have seen the smoke signals many times, and have often asked the blacks what they meant, and have invariably received the explanations promptly. One day I noticed a long way off coil after coil of dark smoke ascending to the upper air, and resembling in its upward motion a spiral staircase. I neglected to count the number of coils, but my black friends did not. On enquiring, "What mean that one, Willie?" I was answered "That one, Moonlight kill 'em galare (emu). Want plenty nunga (men) come. Plenty tucker!" On another occasion a lighter smoke was noticed in the direction of the roast. This was a continuous column interspersed with volumes of dark smoke. I said, "That one black fellow. Micky?" and got the reply, "Oo-ah (yes). Big mob coming alonga coast. Close up, two days Ooldea."

I have experienced another case of the efficiency of the system of smoke signals. I was over at the camp sitting among half a dozen blacks and talking about a sick member of the tribe when suddenly one of them sang out. Immediately all jumped to their feet, yelling out in the native tongue, "Coast mob coming!" Turning to me before he made off, one of the blacks said, "See smoke!" Everywhere excitement reigned supreme, and men, women, boys and girls made for the top of a sandhill and other eminences. The camp was deserted. I was very much amused to see the blacks perched up on branches of trees, like so many bears or birds. After a good look they gradually came down. "Two pfella mob; close up Government taking big coast road," one man told me. "Maybe get here close up dinner time tomorrow!" Although the excitement decreased, the approach of the parties remained a subject of general discussion. "You no answer them, Willie?" I said. "Mucka (no), me no answer. Me make 'em smoke they think we pfellas go to them. They make 'em smoke us, they coming here," he replied. The smoke signal consisted of a big cloud of light smoke. I learnt that visitors have always to signal their approach, and that if they receive no reply they know that all is well, and consequently they come on. If. however, a smoke signal were sent up in reply, it would signify that the mob to whom they had signalled were going to them, and the visitors would then have to await their arrival.

Other signals by pre-arranged smoke columns are used, and that the code of smokes is easily understood, even by the lads and women of the tribe, is quite apparent. The ability of the blacks to select various brush and woods which give different colors and density of smoke is almost uncanny, and no doubt the knowledge has come down through the ages. The various uses to which this method of signalling is put are a striking proof of its efficiency.

The blacks have truly marvellous powers of vision, and no white man that I know of, not even old sea captains, can approach a black in the keenness of eyesight. Out here on the Nullarbor a black can see and point out the smoke of a locomotive some time before it comes within the range of our vision. Time and again I have asked a black, "Is train coming, Jimmy (or whatever his name may be)?" And after a glance the reply is either "Oo-ah (yes)!" or "Mucka (no)"! Should it be "Oo-ah!" and the smoke is not distinguishable by me, he will point out the direction. Sure enough, half an hour later I am able to see the smoke. Frequently one hears, "Here are the blacks! The train must be coming!" Long before the train is due they see the smoke, and come across from their camp in plenty of time.

MEDICINE AND SURGERY. - The blacks are acquainted with the curative properties of various plants, etc., and they are cognisant of the poisonous nature of others. Until quite recently when they learnt the value of the white man's ointments, plasters. and poultices, the blacks used oils made from the fats of goannas and lizards for external sores, whilst for poultices to draw the puss away from festers they used mud. These mud poultices were made with clean earth mixed with warm water to a fairly thick consistency, and the mixture was placed to a thickness of about two inches directly upon the open portion of the sore. It was left in that position for a few days, if the necessities of the case demanded it. After the poultice had been removed, the wound would be cleansed with water if available, and then anointed with the oil obtained from the fat of goannas. The blacks say that these mud poultices are very effective in the object for which they are used. Oils of snakes, lizards, and, in fact, of any animals, are used on the hair of the head for keeping vermin away, etc.

The blacks showed me a peculiar method of curing the irritation caused by the sting or bite of insects, etc., and of removing pimples, itch, and such like. They place in the fire one end of a nice little stick of about an inch in diameter, and when it is well alight they blow out the flame, leaving the end glowing. The bite, itchy part, pimple, or whatever it may be, is then wet with spittle, and the red-hot stick is held as close as possible to it. The drawing action of the heat is immediately experienced, and the itch, etc., disappears.

Very closely resembling our own method of treating snake bite is the one used by the blacks. First a lighted stick is applied to the affected place, then a ligature is tied on each side of the bite and about an inch there-from. Between these two strings the part is cut all round - not only where the bite is, but completely around the leg until the blood flows. They say, "No put 'em string two places finish 'em all up: put 'em string, cut 'em, plenty blood, then balya (good)." A black never kills the snake that bites him, because, in his philosophy, if he lets the snake live he himself will live; but if he kills the snake which has bitten him, well, it's a case of "all finish 'em up." I tried to convince a black of the error of his view, explaining that if he killed the snake all would be well, but if he let the snake escape it might some day come back to finish the job. He, however, stoutly opposed my proposition.

I heard a young black boy crying one day at the top of his voice, and saw him run over to where his father was standing. Some further yells as if the child were suffering pain caused me to go over. I found that the boy had run a large splinter into the fleshy part of his finger, and, to my astonishment, I saw the elder black biting the splinter out. He first gradually worked the splinter to the edge of the skin with his teeth, and having got it thus far he pulled it out with his teeth. It was a rather painful operation for the young boy, but thoroughly successful. The scars seen on the arms, chest, or back of men who have been initiated are the result of incisions made by the initiator with sharp flints reserved for that particular purpose. Excessive bleeding is arrested by applying powdered ashes and cobwebs.

Noticing a black's finger nails exceedingly long, I suggested to him that he should allow me to cut them. He thereupon asked me to do so, and on attempting to clip them with a pair of scissors, I was amazed to find that the scissors would not cut them, the nails being exceedingly brittle. Thinking that this particular black might have been exceptional in this respect, I tried to cut the finger nails of three other blacks, but they were all too brittle, far more so than in the case of any white person that I have seen.

AMUSEMENTS. - There are many and various ways in which the blacks amuse themselves. One favorite way is by means of shadowgraphs. These are made on the walls with their hands, with, of course, a strong light at the back, and the images represent dogs, turkeys, and other kinds of animals and birds. It is very amusing and interesting to see on the wall a representation of a fight cleverly made by the hands and fingers of the blacks. They spend many a pleasant hour during their long nights in this diverting occupation, and several have attained considerable skill in shadowgraphy.

Although no musical instruments are known to the Blacks - if we except the clicking together of two small pieces of wood - it is really remarkable how keenly interested they are in all the musical instruments used by the whites. They grow very enthusiastic over music played for them, and they are not shy in attempting to play themselves, some with much success when one takes into consideration the environment of the blacks. They listen attentively to songs, and have a wonderful faculty for learning the air, particularly of song's or tunes, such as "I Love a Lassie," and I have no doubt but that with training their deep low voices would be heard to advantage in many of the popular songs of to-day. As is well known, their power of imitating the notes of birds, animals, etc., is extraordinary.

The children of the blacks are as fond of playing as our own kiddies are. Indeed, they are eager to play with the white children, and to learn the games that are strange to them. Invariably the black children recognize the leadership of their white companions.

A plaything used by the blacks, and from which the little boys derive considerable enjoyment, is a little wooden cross. It is made from two pieces of light deal or bark, but if procurable three-ply wood is excellent for the purpose, and is eagerly sought after. Care is taken that the pieces are the same in weight and size. One of the pieces of wood has two small slits in the centre of it. Into these slits the second piece of wood is inserted, thus forming a cross. The boy holds the cross in his right hand, and, flipping one end of it with his thumb or finger, gives it a spinning motion, which causes the cross to spin and circle in the air boomerang fashion. The little lads love to jump high and catch the cross as it returns. The purpose of this little plaything is to teach the boys how to catch spinning objects and also to get to understand the action of air-currents.

An amusement of older boys (from 10 to 13 years) is the throwing at each other of small thin pieces of wood resembling miniature spears, but without sharpened points and also without the use of the wommerah (or spear-thrower) to guide the spears and give them speed. These small spears are made from light roots of trees, and they are about three feet long and half-an-inch thick. With these roots they stand approximately a chain apart, and throw them at each other. The boys obtain much amusement from this pastime, for as they close upon each other the dodging becomes more skilful. The object of this pastime is to teach the boys how to throw spears, and how to dodge them, and it is also a training for the eye.

The young boys round about Ooldea make very small boomerangs out of tin, some being only three or four inches long. These they play with by throwing them into the air lightly, and endeavouring to catch them on their return. The tin boomerangs are only intended as playthings, but the blacks bend one edge over so as to resemble the form of the boomerang. The object of this plaything is to illustrate the action of the boomerang, and to show how the air currents affect a boomerang.

The black is remarkable for the aptitude with which he copies the practices of the white man. He adopts the ways of the white man as much as possible because he recognises the superiority of them in many cases over the ones he previously employed. In addition to the good ideas of the whites, the black is particularly apt to acquire the vices, or rather the useless habits, of civilisation. Almost all blacks smoke: swear words are freely used, the black, however, not knowing the meaning of them. But an extraordinary thing is their ability to play games of cards. I have frequently seen half a dozen young native n1en sitting in a circle, and playing such games as Poker, Nap, and Forty-five. Card-playing forms one of their night-time amusements, and by the light of the camp fires they play late into the night. They understand the value of the cards and the points of the game they are playing, and they play in all seriousness. Card games are generally confined to the young "bucks," but very occasionally the women join in. The younger blacks play whenever cards are available; and they frequently ask the white children to obtain playing cards for them. The black is an inveterate gambler, and does not stop at money stakes, for when his money supply is exhausted he will not hesitate to stake his shirt on the result of a game. The young men are also given to playing "two-up." A young black girl had a very good collection of cigarette cards, and with these she and others used to play. They would draw a line and spin a card towards it, in a similar manner to the way the white children play; and afterwards they would toss the cards into the air, after the mode of "two-up."

A THREATENED INVASION. – A few years ago an invasion was threatened by some wild blacks from the North. This caused a considerable amount of excitement among both the whites and the local blacks. The latter prepared for battle, and with full war paint on, they marched up and down throughout the night, singing their war songs. The large camp fires of the enemy were burning brightly a few miles away. The railway pumper at the Soak was camping on his own, and consequently two police and some white volunteers proceeded to his protection. Sure enough, three wild blacks, fully armed, were discovered in the vicinity, and they were captured by the party and brought back to the siding. These three blacks were scouts from the main body of the enemy, and their non-return to the camp apparently alarmed the foe, for they turned and went back to the North.

The three captives were greatly frightened, their teeth chattering and their bodies shivering with fear, for they had never seen white men before. Their condition excited pity from the local blacks who surrounded them, and one stepped forward, took off his coat and shirt, and handed them to a quaking prisoner. Another black immediately offered food. Afterwards the prisoners were taken to the camp of the local blacks, and there warmed, fed and clothed. They were allowed to stay at Ooldea for some week and were then permitted to return to their own country. To say the least, the local blacks were chivalrous and generous to the foe.

WHEN BLACK MEETS BLACK. - A curious custom among the blacks is in evidence when they meet either for the first time or after one has been absent for a considerable period. Should a black arrive at a place where there are other blacks camped, he will sit down and remain seated for at least half an hour before uttering a word. This applies in the case of individuals casually meeting each other, and also when visiting. One day recently a young black who had been away for over twelve months returned from the coast, and although the local blacks saw him and he saw them, not one of them made any movement to go to see him. He on his part lit a small fire and lay down within a couple of hundred yards of the group. I asked one of the blacks to go with me and see who it was, and we went over to him. My friend sat down within six feet of the visitor, but neither of them even looked at each other, nor spoke a word during the time that I was present. In reply to all my questions the visitor answered promptly, and generally conversed with me, but he never once spoke to his brother black, who was still sitting in the same position when I left them. They both lit their pipes at the fire, but no word passed. A new arrival is not allowed to go to the camp until night time, and in some cases he cannot go there until next morning.

"KINGS." - There is no dynasty in the political scheme of the blacks, but there is a tribal leader, and among the whites he is referred to as "King Billy," or whatever his Anglicised name may be. It is the rule that the oldest man of the particular locality is "King" for the time being. Time and again I have noticed that when the very old men have departed: the next oldest man assumes the leadership. The control of the camp and the life thereof is the peculiar and particular province of the King. It is he who decides when and where the camp shall be shifted, and he exercises authority in other directions, particularly in the camp council meetings. The camp council is a very important feature of the communal life of the blacks. The elders sit together and discuss

A type of face. Sambo with a stick through his nose.
A popular form of ornamentation.

various matters affecting their life, and the importance and impressiveness of the council meeting may be gauged from the fact that the women are forbidden even to look in the direction of the meeting, whilst the children are compelled to sit with their backs towards the meeting-place, and to bury their faces in the sand. During the time that the council is in session those left in the camp conduct their conversation in whispers, but when the deliberations are over and the men return to camp the normal tones are resumed.

SHIFTING CAMP. - The blacks shift camp frequently, and they do so for one of many reasons. It may be because of the depletion of food supplies in the neighborhood of the camp, or wood is getting scarce in that locality; perhaps a member of the tribe has died; the general ill-health may necessitate a move on; and so forth. Following upon the death of a young nunga at 2 o'clock one morning, and the burial of the body one hour later, preparations were immediately made to shift camp to a spot some little distance away, despite the fact that it was at 3 o'clock on a bitterly cold morning in July. The blacks were wailing, babies crying, dogs barking, and the camp was a pandemonium. The new camp was a temporary one only. Soon after daybreak more wailing, accompanied by the barking of dogs, was heard; and this signified a fresh move from the temporary camp to a location about a mile away. I watched the process. With long, springing strides the men moved off in Indian file at intervals of about a chain, each carrying his weapons and a few personal belongings. They looked neither to left nor to right. The women followed with bundles on their backs and dogs by their sides, all keeping in single file, and the rear was brought up by the young girls, each carrying all her worldly goods upon her back.

DECORATIONS. - Like every other race of people, white, yellow, red, brown, or black, the Australian aboriginal, male and female, is fond of personal adornment. In many cases the adornment is worn by the men of the tribe only, and more particularly by the young men, who desire to make themselves picturesque. The decoration known to the blacks as book-a-dee, is a case in point. This consists of "skinned" feathers, tied around a small pointed stick, and stuck in the hair as an ornament, and in the making of it the natives embody skill with patience. The large feathers from the wings of birds are obtained, with as many colors as possible. Starting from the top the feathers are taken off each side of the quill in long fine strips. It is fascinating to watch the deftness of the blacks in this feather "skinning," and they are so expert in the operation that not a feather is missed, and not a piece broken. When sufficient feathers have been so treated they are very neatly placed together and wound round and round a small sharp pointed stick, and then tied with a very fine native spun hair, until the whole resembles a neat bundle of feathers of many colors. These bundles are then stuck in the hair and worn generally by the boys. Another decoration is made from a white stick selected for the purpose. The stick is shaved very finely with a piece of glass, and a feather effect is produced. This form of decoration is very popular with lads. Almost every black, male and female, wears a band across the forehead. This band is made of rabbit fur, wombat's fur, human hair, or the wool from an old stocking, and various color effects are produced.

In addition to decorations being placed therein, the hair itself is done up in many ways. For instance, relatives in mourning have their hair cut in a certain manner, and it is a mark of mourning. In the case of a young girl of the Ande-gerrie tribe (in the Tarcoola-Ooldea district) who died, the hair of her relatives was cut very close; but when a man at Ooldea died, the hair was also cut, but not so close.

A peculiar form of ornamentation adopted by the blacks is that of wearing a bone or stick through the cartilage of the nose. The bone-wearing is principally confined to males, and with them it is universal in the males of the tribes frequenting this locality; but a few of the women also affect the ornamentation. The wearing of a bone through the nose is traditional among the blacks, and it is impossible to ascertain when the practice first began and how it came to be introduced. Boys who have passed through the initiation ceremonies invariably wear the bone. There is however, no particular age for the operation of piercing the nose to be performed, nor is any special operator employed to do the job. In fact, many lads do it themselves. The cartilage between the nostrils is pierced with a sharpened piece of wood, and sometimes a spear point is used for the purpose. Through the hole thus made a rounded bone is inserted, and it is left there until the wound is healed, when it may be removed and replaced at leisure. The bone worn through the nose is usually about four or five inches in length, and it is usually obtained from the leg of a wild "turkey," although kangaroo bones and sometimes sticks are used. Yet another ornament greatly fancied by the young men of the tribe is a small tuft of feathers or hair worn in the beard. I have often seen the white fur from the tails of rabbits tied on to the beard of a black. The adoption of this form of ornamentation has no particular significance: it is simply a form of flashness.

THE RIGHT HAND. – We whites are taught from babyhood to use our right hand, and any manifestation by the left is rigorously discountenanced. The result is that we are, generally speaking, a one-handed people. I very much doubt whether this use of the one hand is to our advantage; and from the admiration with which the ambidextrous are held, I would say that it is a decided disadvantage. Now a peculiar thing about the matter is that the blacks, almost without exception, are light-handed, and, so far as I can ascertain, they always have been. Whether the child1en are taught so from babyhood I have not yet satisfied myself upon. Does this use of the right hand by the blacks happen to be a mere coincidence, or is it a survival of the time when man evolved from his anthropoidal ancestors?

The only left-handed black that I know of is a lad named Wong-un-ma, who came to Ooldea from the North recently. This lad is very intelligent, and learnt to speak English in an incredibly short time, and also to write and to draw, the left hand being used. Wong-un-ma, whose photo. appears on a separate page, is a splendid boy of 16 years, and his height is 5 feet 11/2 inches. His district is in the region embraced by Lat. 28-29 and Long. 132-133. The length of his arms, particularly the forearm, is note-worthy. He was a wild black, and had never seen a white person before he came to the line.

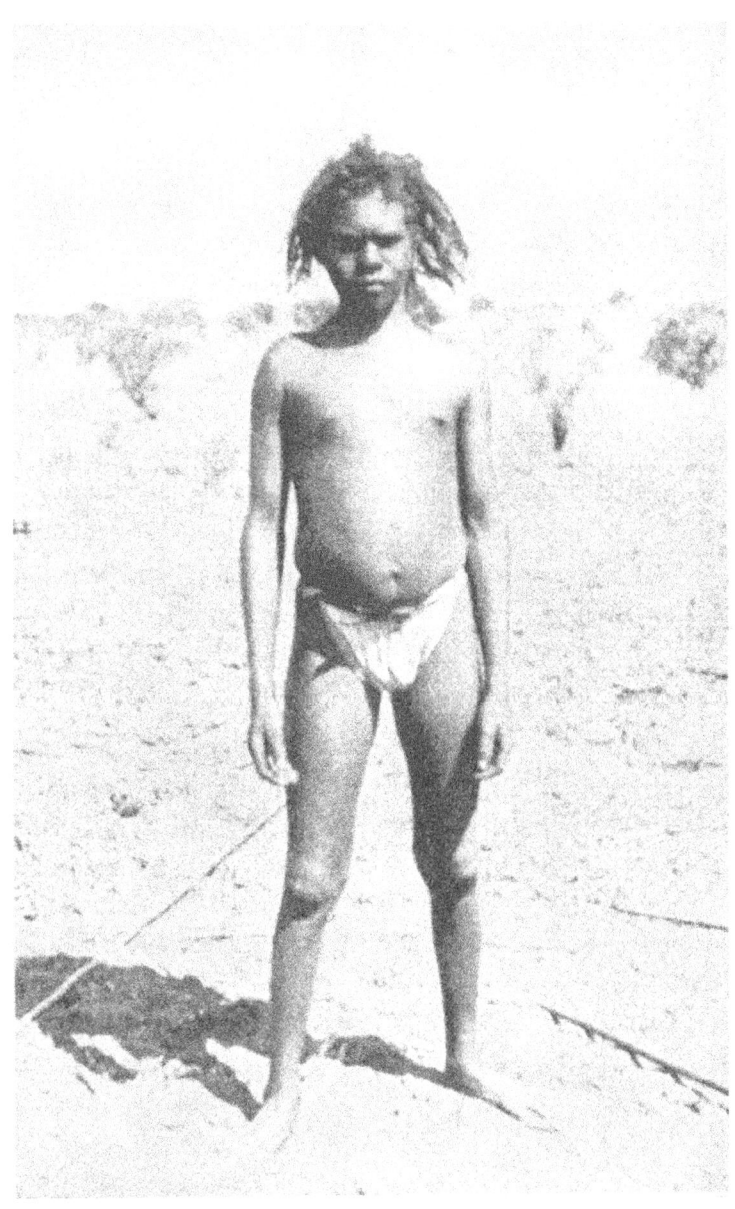

Wong-un-ma. A very intelligent lad, who acquired English in an incredibly short time. Can write his name and draws well, all left hand.

CORROBOREES AND CEREMONIALS. - Dancing and singing appear to be the principal pastimes of the blacks. Many of their dances are performed secretly, and therefore women, children, and uninitiated boys are not permitted to be present, or even to go within a certain distance of the locality where the performances are taking place. They are generally in the nature of sacred ceremonies. On the other hand, there are many other dances, including corroborees, at which women and children sing, as do also the men who are not actually participating in the performance. While singing, the men keep time by beating the ground with stout pieces of wood, or specially prepared waddies. Corroborees are not, as generally supposed, sacred ceremonies; they are really a kind of play, embracing many subjects, and in which the movements of animals, birds, etc., form a prominent feature. The dancers, whilst in the performance, keep perfect time, and exhibit a skill that could have been attained only by long and constant practice. The preparation for a corroboree takes many months to reach the necessary perfection, and during that time the greatest enthusiasm is displayed by all concerned. The corroboree appears to be the second most important event in the life of a black, and it becomes the stadium for his games, the forum for his orations, the palais for his dances, the circus for his contortions, and the platform for his songs. These displays usually start at sunset on moonlight nights, and they continue far into the small hours, and are performed for many nights consecutively, until the climax is reached, when every nerve is strained to its utmost-much in the same way as the grand finale in the modern theatre. The accompanying glare of the fires, the smoky atmosphere, the weird markings on the faces, bodies and limbs of the performers, the ghostly light of the moon, the movements of those participating, the noise of the whole - all these go to produce an uncanny effect, which is most impressive and lasting in the mind of a white, not to mention the influence it would have on those blacks who consider themselves fortunate enough to be present. The corroboree is a performance regarded by the aboriginals with the utmost respect, and not a word is uttered, not even a sound is made, by the onlookers during the whole time it is in operation. Visitors will not be allowed to interrupt the proceedings without much protesting; and, should you be unwise enough to disobey their commands for silence, rest assured no invitation will be extended to you to be present at any more corroborees. These displays travel from tribe to tribe. One may have originated far away in North Queensland, and it would then have been passed on, from tribe to tribe, through the barter routes, until it had traversed the continent, probably taking years to travel down. In July 1920, a display was given at Cook, 86 miles west of Ooldea, in honor of the visit of H.R.H. the Prince of Wales. About sixty blacks were present, and of these twenty were dancers. The performers came from north, east, south, and west, and owing to this fact, it was a difficult task to get the different totem groups to work in harmony. However, the ingenuity of the blacks overcame this difficulty, and a display called the "Yualla" was arranged. The Prince arrived in the day time, and the display lost half of the effect on that account, and through being deprived of the usual atmosphere of smoke. Moreover, a corroboree held in the daytime does not appeal to the mind of the black; and it is a pity that circumstances compelled it to be held when the sun was shining. If the Prince had arrived at Cook, or, preferably, at Ooldea, in the night, he would have witnessed a performance which, I am sure, would have compared very favorably with any of the many native dances and displays witnessed by him during his wonderful trips. However, His Royal Highness, after witnessing the performance, expressed himself as follow: -

"I am interested and delighted with the primitive performance, and the actual aboriginal avocations of fur-spinning, flint-sharpening, seed-crushing, fire-making, etc. I feel that I have witnessed a most unique performance, and one that I shall probably never see again."

The swinging of the Koondain (the sacred "bull- roarer") by the young natives who had just passed through their initiation ceremony, was perhaps the most unique part of the display; and it is doubtful whether white men will ever be permitted to see it again. The Prince, at the termination of the display, was presented by each native with a weapon, as a memento of the occasion, and a good representative collection was thus obtained. The principals in charge of the display presented him with a wommerah and a boomerang, both inscribed, the inscription on the wommerah being: "Booneri Ngalli Yanning Nyinning!" (Master coming; glad to see him; welcome!), and on the boomerang: "Wanyu Ngalla Ulbin!" (Come back again soon!)

CEREMONIES. - Sacred ceremonies are quite different from corroborees, and they vary very considerably with different tribes. They are by far the most important events in the life of an aboriginal. These ceremonies are extremely sacred, and the care taken to ensure the secretness of the proceedings is remarkable. Scouts are placed in all directions, and no woman, child or uninitiated youth is allowed to venture within a mile of the selected spot. These ceremonies are the only ones of which a black will give no information. They are so important that tribes gather from near and far. In the particular case of which I have knowledge, they came from Fowler's Bay (129 miles southwards), Tarcoola and Kingoonya (217 miles to the east), and Karonie and Kalgoorlie (624 miles westwards). The ceremony lasted for seven days, being almost continuous, day and night. The members of a foreign tribe are always the operators in one of these ceremonies, the Kalgoorlie men officiating in the one now under review. Four youths were initiated into manhood. These boys were selected some time previously - the exact time is not known, but it ran into a few months - and, after undergoing preparation, they were isolated, and were subsequently conveyed from the place of isolation to the scene of operation. After the initiation ceremony they were again isolated, and supplied with the sacred instrument called the "bull-roarer." This is a small instrument that makes a peculiar buzzing noise when whirled through the air; and, should anyone intrude near the place of ceremony, the "bull-roarer" is brought into use, and it is then supposed to bring all kinds of serious illness and trouble upon the offender. The initiated youths next appear in public with their hair wound up in a big bun, which is tied on the rear portions of their heads. This bun arrangement is sometime made up from other material, woven in with the hair. About this time a bone is worn through the nose; but this bone-wearing is probably only a form of ornamentation, and is not confined to the period immediately following upon the initiation. There are two operations - circumcision and sub-incision - included in the ceremony. They may be performed separately, but if the candidate be old enough for both operations to be carried out at the one time, that is done. The actual operation is done very skilfully and quickly, with specially-prepared flints, which are used solely for that purpose. Excessive bleeding is stopped by the use of wood ashes.

There is much evidence to prove that when a young black says "Me nunga" (I am a man) he means much more than the mere words convey. To be able to say that, he has had to pass the initiation ceremonies, and the torture and suffering associated with the function have had to be borne unflinchingly by him. Should the boy fail to bear the pain without crying he is unfitted for manhood, and consequently will not have the opportunity of learning from his elders the sacred laws and rites of his tribe. The scars he bears represent the totem of his particular tribe.

MESSAGE STICKS. - When a sacred ceremony is about to take place, the members of a tribe are called together wherever they may be. One of the means employed is the message stick, of which there are many in existence, and the blacks used to make extensive employment of them. These sticks are of various lengths, widths, and designs, but the usual length is somewhere in the vicinity of seven inches. They are either round or flat, and their surface is covered with carved lines, dots or squares, but in a good many cases the lines, dots or squares are burnt into the wood. When a messenger is sent with a stick, he is, of course, conversant with the nature of the communication, and, on arrival at his destination, he would be capable of explaining the message, the stick, in this case, constituting a compliment from one chief to another. The real test of the ability of a black to interpret a message is made when a stranger carries the stick. Previous to the last initiation ceremony at Ooldea, a messenger was sent to Kalgoorlie, and delivered his stick. The message ran: "Kalgoorlie tribe very much late. Ooldea tribe very anxious; getting restless. What is reason of delay?" The return stick bore the following reply: "Yes, we've been coming long time, but Government will not allow us travel on train. Much late, but still come on." A much more critical test was made a few months later. Some ceremony was to be performed at Karonie, 60 miles east of Kalgoorlie, and, as a few Karonie blacks were in the Ooldea district, they were wanted back. The problem was to send a messenger so far in such hot weather, and particularly as he would have to "foot" it, a matter of about 600 miles, owing to the black being prohibited from travelling, unless he paid his fare, which, of course, was impossible. The Karonies thereupon decided to send a message stick by a white man on the "Tea and Sugar," a weekly train that traverses the line, delivering groceries, bread, meat, wood, water, etc. This man refused to carry the stick unless the Karonies explained the message to him, so that he could test the ability of the Ooldea blacks to interpret it on arrival. In the presence of some whites, the messenger handed the stick to an Ooldea black, and said: "Well, what say that one?" After close scrutiny, the black replied: "Take alonga Wynbring. They been want 'em Lame Charlie and Big Peter. All Karonie nunga go back big corroboree!" The stick was rounded, and was about one inch in diameter and seven inches in length. A snake's head was carved at one end, and the other was tapered to a medium-sized point. There were lines and dots on the stick - some half-a-dozen dots, a few lines the full length of the stick, and about a dozen lines running round the stick. The dots and lines were all burnt into the stick: and there were no other decorations of any kind.

WRITING. – The ability of the black to recognise the superiority of the white man's method is proved by his discarding the message stick and utilising paper instead, then sending the note by the engine-driver, guard, passenger, or even in very isolated cases per medium of the mail bag (the envelope being addressed by a white). The symbols are written on the paper instead of being carved on the stick. With very little practice the black become an adept in writing, and the "paper message sticks" are in much more common use than is generally realised. The blacks write and interpret the messages without hesitation or difficulty. The written messages have been known to contain requests for food, enquiries about sickness, displays, etc.; and it is quite feasible to assume that as the black realises the value of writing he will make greater use of it, and a regular system of correspondence will be established. Believe me, many of them foresee such a development. The days of the carved message sticks are therefore rapidly becoming a thing of the past; in fact I will go so far as to say that they are not now in use. Their writings open up a great field of investigation for the student. I have given the matter a lot of attention, and I find that whilst some of the symbols are common there are others the meaning of which is known only to the particular tribe. It is presumed from this that each tribe has some secret markings or symbols, the meaning thereof being known only to and jealously guarded by the elders. The following incident was related to me by Driver W. Morgan of Ooldea: "One day Fat Mickey (Win-a-mar) came to my camp and wanted to write a message to Charlie. This Charlie had recently been working on Wilgena Station, and had apparently 'cashed-up,' so Mickey thought he would get some things sent along. A pencil and a piece of paper were given to Mickey, who thereupon made certain curves and crosses, the appearance of the whole being similar to the representation of a streak of lightning. I informed Mickey that unless he told me what he had written I would refuse to take the message. He told me the contents. Charlie had not heard from Mickey, nor did he know that I had a letter for him until I arrived at Tarcoola, 180 miles from Ooldea. On handing the message to Charlie at Tarcoola, I said "What say that letter?" Charlie replied: "Mickey say he hungry pfella; want me send him alonga you flour, sugar, tea, 'bacca. and bullets, 44 rifle." Sure enough, that agreed with what Mickey had told me before I left Ooldea.

THE FOOD OF THE BLACKS. - The black is no gastronomer. All that comes his way is food, and within the range of dingo and grub he has a vast variety to choose from. One of the choicest morsels in his larder is a cream-colored grub called a "Bardy"; and this he eats without any culinary preparation. Such things as dingoes, snakes, goannas, kangaroos, rabbits, bandicoots. emus, turkeys, mallee fowl, and birds generally he grills before eating; but as long as the fur, feathers, or skin is burnt off - well, that's near enough! In the season, he eats the native peach (or quondong) and the mulga apple, two of the fruits indigenous to this part of the world. In ability to secure food, the black stands on a pinnacle by himself. Endowed by Nature with wonderful eyesight and with an extraordinarily acute hearing, the black is eminently fitted to be a hunter. In addition to those faculties, he is rapid and silent in his movements, and being a born naturalist he knows the habits and the location of his victims as no-one else does. A black would not waste time digging out a useless burrow in the hope of securing, say, a bandicoot or a reptile. He first of all traces the object of his search to its burrow or hole, and no matter what the animal may be, he can say with unfailing accuracy the exact place where the animal or reptile is, and very often, how many he will obtain, and approximately their ages. His wonderful knowledge of nature guides him with such certainty, that all useless searching is eliminated, and the object of his quest is quickly obtained by digging direct on to it. Scattered over the countryside are innumerable examples of hunting by the blacks; and once seen they are so easily distinguishable from the laborious efforts of the white man.

TRACKING. - In this country, where Nature has endowed most of the animal, reptile, and insect life with protective covering to harmonise with the surroundings. and where each living thing is the food of something else, the securing of food would under ordinary circumstances be a difficult matter for a white man. Not so with the black. Their wonderful power of hearing is surpassed only by their marvellous eyesight. Their ability as trackers is known throughout the world; but to be appreciated it must be seen. What is hidden to but very few whites is an open book to the black. The displacement of the smallest object, the slightest indent in the soil, a broken twig, a microscopic scratch on a rock - all tell him something, and his interpretation is invariably correct. With them tracking is a profession. In the early days of infancy the blacks are taught to track ants; and they are also encouraged in the study of animals and their habits. It is no wonder then that the black tracker is a necessary adjunct to every police force; these sable sons of the soil make splendid Sherlock Holmeses. Their ability as trackers makes the securing of food an easy matter, and their power of mimicry of voice and movement is an additional help in this direction.

The blacks can tell at a glance whether a footprint was made by a male or by a female, and after a closer examination to whom it belongs. They know every track in the bush, how old any track is, whether it was made by a young or old animal, whether the animal was tired or fresh, and frequently the quest of the animal.

"You want me, Missa Bolam?" asked Freddie, a young nunga. "Yes," I replied; "I sent Mickey for you. I want you to come with me in the sulky and find dingo. Last night a dingo got in my rabbity trap, and ran away with it on his leg. I track him long way this morning, but lose 'em: too hard white pfella track him. You come alonga me, eh?"

"Oo-ah!" replied the hunter. "Righto I jump up here, and we will drive out to where I lost the tracks." On arrival at the spot (which I had marked), I handed over control to Freddie. Before starting he asked many questions as to how far the dingo had come, what his last tracks were like (curving or straight, etc.); and on receiving the information he remarked, "Pup-bah (dingo) not go very far; must be close up: by-bye leg swell, and he sleep 'em then"; and pointing ahead Freddie indicated the way the dingo would go. The track was now at least 24 hours old, and in the meantime a sand storm had come along, and obliterated it. In the morning I lost the track in dry, stony, and hard country. It was a revelation to see how the black set about his task, and his knowledge of the dingo's habits was amazing. Pointing right ahead he slowly made off, myself and a friend following in the sulky. About 80 yards on he observed an upturned stone, remarking, "That pup-bah alright; chinna (foot) kick 'em stone." There was no more hesitation: a stone upturned here and there, a piece of grass or bluebush broken now and again, a leaf or a dry twig disturbed, all were pointed out. The country now became more soft and sandy, and showed that the dingo had crossed from the plain to the sandhills. In the sand the tracks were easily followed; and the tracker remarked, "Rabbity trap on front chinna; pup-bah run along three legs, no drop trap"; which meant that the trap was on one of the dingo's front legs, and he was holding it up, and running on three legs. Coming to a place where the dog had lain down, Freddie said, "Tired pfella; him sleep here. He hear us coming, jump up and run away!" Then correcting himself, he remarked, "Mucka! (no!); we no frighten him. Another blackfellow come this way. You see 'em tracks? He track pup-bah now!" "Do you know whose tracks they are?" I asked. "Oo-ah!" he replied, after carefully scrutinising them, "They are Yarrie's!" We followed on, and came to the spot where Yarrie had killed the dingo with a waddy, and thrown the carcase under a tree. Everything that happened during the kill was explained to us by Freddie from the footprints. Here Yarrie had sprung out, there he had first hit the dingo, to this place he had followed and struck the dingo again, there the dingo had moved, and struggled. In fact, the black read from his book of signs, and we followed the lesson with great interest. On the following morning Yarrie made his appearance, carrying the rabbit trap and the dingo's scalp. He explained that he had seen the tracks, followed them, and killed the animal.

Tracking is extensively used by the blacks in their search for food. Such ground animals and reptiles as leave marks during movement are tracked to their underground homes, and then dug out. Rabbits, bandicoots, foxes, dingoes are all tracked down to their resting-places, and captured. Snakes, lizards, etc., are also tracked and dug out from their haunts, if not previously killed. The tracking of a snake presents many difficulties to white bushmen, as it is hard to determine in which direction the snake has travelled. But the blacks have no such difficulty. They note that a snake generally leaves a slightly larger amount of dirt on one side as it twists about, and this gives the clue as to the direction in which it is travelling. If this indication be not present, the blacks closely scrutinise the tracks, and knowing that the tail leaves a narrower trail than the body they get the direction from that fact. Even this indication is extremely difficult to observe in hard rocky country; but the black will master it. I well recollect that on one particular occasion the track of a large snake was observed near our home on a summer morning; and it caused some little concern in our household. To allay the feelings of my wife, I requested Tommy, one of the blacks from here, to find the reptile. Tommy set to work straightaway, and the snake was tracked from a truck of wood, which had been recently unloaded, to right under the house, thence to a water-trough, and from there under a shed, and out again, then right away for a quarter of a mile into a small burrow, where Tommy dug it out and despatched it.

The tracking of animals possessing legs is not so difficult for the blacks, but it is quite difficult enough in hard stony country. On one occasion a young mouse with young attached to the teats escaped during the night from a cage in which I had it confined. As it was about to be forwarded to the Adelaide University for biological purposes, I was most anxious to recapture it, and accordingly I offered a black a reward to recover it. Off he started. Its every movement from the cage (and, as may be supposed, there were many) was carefully followed, until the track leading out into the bush was located. From there onwards for a few hundred yards rapid progress was made, for the country was slightly sandy; but a little further on hard limestone was met with. From this point the black kept his eyes riveted to the ground ahead, never for the slightest fraction of a second removing them from the track. Being at one stage unable to see any mark whatever, I asked Bobby to instruct me. He pointed out two yards ahead where a very small stone had been slightly moved, also a broken leaf. These explanations resulted in the black losing for the time being the faint track. To pick it up again, he commenced making a series of small circles, then gradually widened them until in one soft place he again picked up the track. Before the inevitable burrow was eventually located, the track was lost on two more occasions, but the same circling movement enabled it to be picked up again; and ultimately the object of our quest was located in a burrow and recaptured. The tracking was carried out for considerably more than a mile, and over much difficult hard limestone country.

On another occasion my wife lost a brooch which, on account of the sentiment associated with it, was regarded as being of considerable value. She and every other available white were pressed into searching for it, but without result. Later on in the day a black came along, and I immediately got him on the job. The following dialogue ensued: -

White: "Toby, my white lubra lose 'em brooch. You find 'em, me been pay you two bob, and give you dry tea and supper."

Black: "Which way lose 'em?"

White: "I don't know, but somewhere in the camp, and not too far away."

Black: "Oo-ah (yes)! I been find 'em close up soon. This one boota wear 'em when lose 'em?" (pointing to the lady's boot).

White: "No; different one."

Black: "You show 'em me which one boota wear 'em when lose 'em brooch."

I produced my wife's shoe, and Toby, after selecting a clean sandy patch, made a neat impression of the foot and heel, and then handed back the shoe. Down on his hands and knees, Toby carefully studied the impression, and saying, "I been find 'em close up!" he started off on his important mission. Sitting on the doorstep, I eagerly watched the movement of the black. Backwards and forwards he went, sometimes at a quick pace, at other times very slowly, but with eyes ever looking a few yards ahead. Nothing was missed by him from the time my wife left home until she returned. In front of the local railway station, trodden into the sand by the numerous footsteps that had passed over the spot, the brooch was recovered. Passengers from two trains and the local whites had walked over the spot many times, but notwithstanding this, Toby's sharp eyes had followed my wife's track to the end, noting where she stood, turned, moved quickly or slowly, and every other incident of her walk.

So that the reader may better appreciate this wonderful ability to track anything at all, I will relate a couple of instances in which I was personally involved, and in doing so I shall adhere to the dialogistic form.

Another type of face. This man, Jimmy (Jagella) died recently, see page 74.

White: "Hullo, Sambo, what are you doing out here?"
Black: "Lose 'em rabbity; me track 'em close up!"
White: "I see, tracking rabbit, eh?"
Black: "Oo-ah! (yes!)"
White: "You teach me track too?"
Black: "Oo-ah!"
White: "Righto! Off we go then!"

Circling round from where a rabbit had been squatting, Sambo suddenly found a mark made in a patch of sand by a stone. This was the only mark visible, as the rest of the ground all around was exceedingly hard country. Thisone mark, however, was all that was required, for Sambo had obtained the direction. Sambo now arose and stood quite still with wrinkled brow, and peered ahead for quite half a minute; and to me it was evident that he was reckoning out the animals movements from that particular spot. Keen eyesight in such a case was an essential, but a knowledge of the habits of the animal, and the power of deduction was equally necessary. Suddenly Sambo moved off, and without the slightest hesitation he made for some unknown object, following no tracks. As we proceeded, his objective became apparent. It was a rabbit's burrow about two hundred yards away. Arriving at the warren, Sambo was soon down on hands and knees, and after minutely examining the mouth of the burrow he remarked, "Rabbity sit down inside. You see 'em?" "No, I don't," I replied. Sambo continued, "This one, chinna (foot); this one; and this one!" illustrating his words by pointing out tracks going into the burrow. "Yes, I see the tracks now," I said; "but how you tell which way they go?" "Easy fellow that one; you see 'em chinna mark cornildatta (all the same)?" "Oh, yes! Now I see foot mark all same, toe nail going this way, eh?" "Balya, oo-ah! (good, yes!)" said Sambo. From the marks made by the toe nails of the rabbit, as well as by the pad of the foot, Sambo could easily make out the direction.

Here is another instance of tracking by another black:-
White: "Nanny-goat lose 'em picaninny! You find em?"
Black: "Oo-ah!"
White: "She come home drink water, leave 'em juga-juga along bush!"

Black: "Oo-ah, I know. How long lose 'em?"
White: "Three days now, coogearra cooge-ha (three)!"
Black: "Which way lose 'em?"
White: "I'm sure I can't tell you, Jackie. I never saw her come home."
Black: "Comenpanye close up finish juga-juga (hot sun nearly kill the little one)!"
White: "Yes. You look this way (pointing to south) first time. Come back dinner time, and see me!"
Black: "Balya, oo-ah (good, yes)."

When dinner time came around, Jackie returned without the kid, but with the remark. "No see 'em that way. Must be that way (pointing to the north)!" To which I replied, "I'll go with you after dinner."

The meal over we set out for the sand-hills, and we had not proceeded far, when Jackie said:
Black: "Picaninny track this way, but old pfella (baby track here, but this is an old one)!"
White: "How old that track, eh?"
Black: "Mucka, close up four day (not sure, but about four days)."
White: "How you tell four days old?"
Black: "Big pfella wil-ba man-goora (I see big wind four days ago, and these tracks were made before that)."

That was an eye-opener to me: the tracking is read with the aid of common-sense reasoning. Quite a number of tracks were found that had leaves or sand blown into them, and hardened excreta was come across. These proved how long ago the kids had gone that way. The tracks were all passed over without further attention; but they served their purpose by indicating the locality in which to search. After we had traversed some distance, success at last crowned our efforts, for Jackie had struck fresh tracks, remarking, "Juga-juga cooge-arra: no muder, only juga- juga (little one, two; no mother, only little ones)!
White: "How old track?"
Black: "One day, mucka (no) more!"
White: "You find 'em now?"

Black : "Oo-ah, close up. Little one sick!"

For another half a mile we followed the tracks, every incident of interest being pointed out to 1ne by Jackie, such as "Sit down here!" "Play about here!" etc., until near the end of our search Jackie said, "Minga (sick) pfella all time sit down!" A little distance further on we found the two little kids snuggled under a tree, and almost perishing from want of food.

The ability to track is not confined to the men and boys, but the lubras are also clever at it. On one occasion Mrs. Bolam and the baby went for a walk with another lady; and as the day was rather warm they rested in the shade of a native peach tree on the side of a sandy slope. The child pulled a brooch out of her mother's blouse; and its absence was not detected until sometime after. Then the two ladies made a diligent search, but could find no trace of the brooch, as it had become covered with sand. On arrival home my wife sent a black gin to look for it, and it wasn't long before the gin returned with the brooch. She had tracked them right down to the sandhill, and located the missing article.

On another occasion a gin was given a parcel of food by a passenger on the train, and she walked away a few yards and placed it on a box. Another passenger thought he would play a joke on Polly, and accordingly while she was posing for a photo. he slipped around, picked up the parcel, and hung it on a tree about a chain away. When Polly turned around to get her parcel, she found it missing; but without any hesitation she picked up the joker's tracks, followed them to the tree, obtained her parcel, followed the tracks back to the culprit, and turned the joke on him.

On one occasion 1 said to a black, "You been get 'em that one, eh, Tommy?" "Oo-ah (yes)," replied Tommy; "me been track 'em close up!" Tommy was examining some marks on the slope of a hill, and they were the recently-made tracks of a dingo. "That one track old pfella goolga pup-bah (old female dog). By-bye big pfella sleep all the time, sleep plenty. Me catch 'em sleep, then spear 'em!" he said. "Ah, I see," said I. "Well, how far go away?" "Close up may be tindoo," pointing to the sun, which was then about the zenith.

"Well, I will come," I said. Off we went. Whilst we were on the hill side with the wind in our face, the track was followed without any danger, but presently the track turned, and the wind was with us. After studying the position for a few minutes, Tommy decided that the dingo had continued over the hill, and that it would be useless to follow the track, as the wind would blow his scent along to the animal. To overcome the difficulty, Tommy set off in movements resembling the shape of a boomerang, picking up the track, but only for a moment, every now and then. On and on we go, until at last he explains quietly, "Close 'up now, fresh tracks just made. Soon be see 'em pup-bah (dingo)!" Tommy then beckoned 1ne to stay behind and make no noise, whilst he began stalking the enemy. The silence was so intense that the slightest noise could have been heard. After proceeding thus for about 100 yards Tommy stopped, and from my position I could see him taking off his shirt and trousers. I climbed to a bit of a knoll, and was greatly interested in the hunt. On went the hunter with nothing except spear and wommerah. Another 50 yards was carefully negotiated, and Tommy stopped under a tree with a fork in it, over which he cautiously peeped. During the last 600 yards not a twig was broken, not the slightest sound was made. I was beginning to get restless with the waiting, yet I was afraid of moving for fear of breaking the silence. Presently I saw Tommy steadily raise his spear and wommerah into position for throwing, then a sudden bound, and in the twinkling of an eye the spear was hurled with great force, and immediately there was a piercing animal cry as the spear ran through the dingo, an exultant yell from the hunter, a rush, a few smashing blows from the wommerah across the neck of the transfixed animal, a gurgling noise, and then quietness. As I rushed up, I noticed the triumphant look of a victorious warrior on Tommy's face. An inspection of the dingo showed me that the spear had struck her on the side, had passed through the body, and was protruding over a foot on the other side. It was a thrilling experience for me, and I gloried in the combat between the skill of my black friend and the natural cunning of the dingo, an animal that would yield nothing, not even to the fox, in a battle of wits.

The dialogue was then continued: -
White: "Why such a long wait, Tommy?"
Black: "Pup-bah (dingo) all-a-time keep moving. By-by rest alonga tree; then spear 'em!"
White: "Oh, I see, all the time move about; you wait till he tired, and rest,"
Black: "Ooh-ah (yes)!"
White: "Why take 'em off clothes?"
Black: "Trousers all time make 'em noise: no good, nunga (blackfellow) want 'em free!"
White: "I see. Trousers rub together, make 'em noise, and when off, give you free use of legs, eh?"
Black: "Oo-ah!"

PROCURING WATE R. – Water, a difficult problem to the white man in this county - and what terrible torments from thirst did those immortal explorers endure in their journeys into the interior - the blacks know how and where to procure, whether it be in gnamma holes, native wells, soaks, native dams, caves or trees. It, will be remembered that Giles, in 1875, found a dam made by the blacks near the boundary between Western Australia and South Australia, and named by him "Boundary Dam." Earlier in that year, Giles came across a circular wall or dam of clay built by the blacks at Pylebung (between Ooldea and Wynbring). This dam was 20 yards long, nearly 5 feet thick at the bottom, and 2 feet at the top. It was made by the blacks with small wooden shovels. Others have come across wells many feet in depth, which the blacks have scraped out to reach water. Native wells are to be found here and there in the beds of creeks and in the sand along the shore of the Great Australian Bight. Eyre, you will recollect, after journeying 150 miles from the last water, and when death was daily dogging his and Wylie's footsteps, found a place on the sandy shore where the blacks had dug for water. As I have described elsewhere, the blacks can always obtain water from the roots of the brown-bark mallee and from oak trees.

CANNIBALISM. - There is unchallengeable proof that cannibalism has been resorted to by some blacks; but the natives round about Ooldea are ashamed of the fact, and they have studiously endeavored to conceal the knowledge of it from the white man. A case of cannibalism occurred so recently as October 1920, at Ooldea itself, as Mrs Daisy Bates can testify. But it is a gruesome subject, and one best left undescribed. To come across an isolated instance or two of cannibalism having been resorted to by a black is no proof that it was practised by the blacks, and is no justification for the blacks being described as "cannibals"; just as it would be absurd for the English to be so described because a gang of convicts who escaped from Macquarie Harbor (Tasmania) less than 100 years ago killed and ate each other.

CHARACTER - My experience of the blacks enables me to speak of them in the most favorable terms. There are many and indisputable proofs on their part of the possession of a very high sense of humanity. Here is an instance of honesty on the part of a black which would put to sham e ninety-nine out of every hundred whites, and as I was present at the time, I vouch for the accuracy of what I relate. During the construction of the Trans-Australian Railway, the Department ran stores at various places along the line, as it still does. One of these stores was situated at Ooldea. One day a "nunga" called Charlie, who had acquired some of the arts of civilisation, presented himself to the store, and wanted to buy some tobacco. The money he tendered was a shilling short, and the storeman (who at stocktaking had to account for the stock or the cash) demurred at supplying him. Said Charlie, "Me be wantem 'bacca; you been lend 'em me, and me bl'ing 'em money back by-by!" The storeman, having: faith in his "black brother of the bush," let him have a plug of the fragrant weed, and Charlie went off happy. Next day, Charlie's tribe left the district, and the storeman paid in the "bob," and in the hustle and bustle of business he gradually forgot all about the incident. Ten months later, a black walked into the store, and said to the storenman, "Me been owe 'em you bob long time ago; you been give 'em me 'bacca; me now pay." And to the astonished storeman Charlie paid his shilling and departed. Charlie told me later that he had earned some money alonga coast, and not being able to pay earlier, he had returned specially to liquidate his debt - a mere jaunt of 125 miles or so on foot through country that is nearly waterless. Mr. Tietkens, who was out here with Giles in 1875, writing to me concerning his own exploration towards the Musgrave Ranges in 1878, relates the following instance of the reliability and loyalty on the part of a black: -

"A black used to carry my letters to Fowler's Bay. I put them in a forked stick, and said, 'Paper Yabber Yalata' (Yalata is the homestead station near Fowler's). and off he went without a word or a rag on his back, and brought my mail back, saying, 'Paper yabber' - that was all the English he had. The police at Fowler's Bay at my request gave him a day or two spell and a shirt. He returned all right, but with no shirt. I had nothing to give him, and he didn't seem to expect anything. No water on that one hundred odd miles, except Pidinga (a rock- hole about midway between Ooldea and Fowler's Bay). It was a wonderful service."

You who travel by the Trans-Australian across the 1051 miles of country with no visible surface water, will be able to realise the value of such a demonstration of loyalty by a black to his white chief. But Australian history is full of such incidents.

The blacks in their trading are scrupulously fair, and they quickly realise the various values of our coinage. If a black were in your debt, and he subsequently earned some money from you for a service performed, it would never do for you to say to him, "You been owe 'em me iso much; here is the balance!" Such a thing would to his idea be tantamount to no payment at all. He would expect to be paid in full, and would then hand you back what he owed. Unless it passed from his hands to yours, he would consider that he still owed you the money.

Despite the cruelty to which the nunga subjects his lubra, the fidelity of the woman is remarkable. A nunga beats his lubra with a waddy, kicks her, and generally bashes her about, and at the same time, he makes her do all the work. In return for this cruel treatment he gets faithfulness and loyalty. This loyalty was on one occasion expressed in a most amusing way. A black was taken to a hospital suffering from appendicitis. His lubra went to see him. When the nurse's back was turned, the lubra got into bed alongside of him; but of course, was driven out on the nurse's return immediately afterwards. Several times this happened, until the lubra was forbidden entry to the ward. The lubra considered it was her place to serve her master, no matter where he happened to be, and her place was by his side.

RELIGIOUS BELIEFS. - In our sense of a God they have none; nor have they any religion such as we practise. They are, however, intensely superstitious, and have an almost unshakeable belief in the powers of evil spirits, magic, etc. Indeed, every mishap is attributed to sorcery. If, through contact with the whites for any length of time, they waver in their belief in the powers of the evil spirits, their faith is quickly renewed when they return to their wild life. During recent years much discussion has taken place as to whether the blacks believe in a Supreme Being, and it has been strongly argued pro and con. Those whites who have lived among the blacks, or those who, like myself, have been admitted into their inner confidence, are firm in the conviction that they do not subscribe to a belief in the Grand Architect of the Universe; but the blacks are convinced of the existence of a Supernatural Being that exercises an evil influence only. All happenings, such as illness, accidents, thunder, lightning, storms of all kinds, and other harmful occurrences are manifestations of the power of the Evil One. Accordingly during heavy atmospheric disturbances, the black exhibit symptoms of fear, and rarely show themselves outside of their wurleys. Mr. W. H. Tietkens tells n1e that when he was at Ooldea in 1878, an eclipse of the sun occurred early in the afternoon. There was a crowd of blacks about, some of them not too good; and he erected a line of brush all around his tent, and none was allowed within the quarter-acre enclosure. When the eclipse occurred the women and children came crying and screaming with fear, broke down the barrier, and made for his tent. The men followed, their teeth chattering from fear. The tent was soon packed with women and children with the men

all around. The women were crying out "Tyn-do pooh; tyn-do pooh!" (sun gone). Their belief in evil spirits is shown in no unmistakeable manner during and after burial ceremonies. When a burial is taking place, a fire is lighted near the grave (in some cases right in the grave), so that the evil spirits may warm themselves without visiting the camp fires. After the burial, a fire is kept going near the grave, and also between the grave and the camps, which are generally immediately shifted to some new location. This is for the same reason as mentioned above. For many nights after the burial a great wailing is set up in the camp, and continues till far into the night; the object being to appease or frighten the evil spirits from the camp. There are no traces of idolatry being practised by the tribes at Ooldea, nor have I ever had any reason to believe that the practice ever existed. Images the blacks certainly have, but they are of a very rude kind, and generally hideous, and have no religious aspect at all. Contrary to the assertions of some writers, I can say that the blacks pay no respect to, or have no reverence for, old age; and there is no evidence of ancestor-worship, veneration for the dead, or, indeed, of any such things customary with the whites. In July, 1920, a display by aboriginals was given at Cook, on the Trans-Australian Railway, in honor of the visit of His Royal Highness the Prince of Wales. In the camp was a friendless old woman. Being old, she was not wanted by anyone, and although repeated efforts were made to put her in the others' wurleys, she was time after time turned out in the bitter cold. No respect was paid to her old age, and as a consequence of the treatment to which she was subjected, she died the day after the Prince passed through, and she now lies buried close by the little graveyard at Cook. Cases have been known where the old and feeble members of a tribe who were no longer of use, but rather a hindrance to the others, were taken to a far-away water-hole, and the younger members of the tribe, on the pretext that they were going hunting, abandoned the decrepit. Still we must not judge the blacks too harshly on this account, because the circumstances of their nomadic existence are such that only the useful is wanted. The dead, however, are never mutilated, nor are their graves desecrated in any way. This apparent respect for the dead does not arise from veneration, but from fear of the evil spirits which frequent the locality. The blacks never speak of the dead except in low tones, fer they believe that if they spoke loudly the evil spirit would think they were not sufficiently sorry for the dead person and would therefore get very angry, and evil times would surely follow. I once said to a black, whose lubra had died recently, "Lindy all finish, Georgie?" He replied in low tones, almost a whisper, "Hush! Oo-ah (yes) all finish up!" It does not do to speak loudly of any dead person in the presence of a black, as one may frighten him very badly.

When asked the reason for any of their old sacred customs, the blacks cannot explain, but answer simply, "Mucka me!" (I don't know). Their oppressive laws and customs belong to a tremendously remote past, and the origin of, and reason for them are hidden in the haze of antiquity. To-day, after long and close questioning, I can get from them nothing better than, "We have always done it: it was our father's custom, and so it is our's to-day!" Still, that peculiarity is not confined to the Australian aboriginal.

The blacks do not speak of a Hereafter; but they have some faint idea of metempsychosis, because cases are known of whites, from their supposed resemblance to some deceased aboriginal, or of their being found asleep on the grave of an aboriginal, being called by the deceased's name. This seems to indicate that they believe to some extent in the transmigration of souls.

IN LIGHTER VEIN. - The black is a born comedian, and he is also easily amused, anything with a touch of humor in it provoking from him roars of a laughter which is by no means unpleasant. The black is naturally in his native element a happy care-free fellow who is either whistling a tune or humming some song. He appreciates a joke at his own or the other fellow's expense, and as a "leg-puller" he has few equals. Nowadays the Department sends an operator along the line with a Pathe Home Cinema, and when the pictures are screened at a station where the blacks are camped, the most popular items are those of the Charlie Chaplin type.

The following incidents are not devoid of a humorous side: -

Two contractors each employed a black to cut firewood at Ooldea for departmental purposes, and the day was one of those occasions when the mercury almost sizzles in the thermometer. One black, fairly knocked out, lies in the shade of a small tree. The other black, although not employed by the sleeping beauty's boss, does not believe in the other fellow snoring while he himself is toiling, and so he tries to wake him up. After several attempts, he fails to arouse the slumberer, and walks away disgusted. Not satisfied, however, he returns in a little while, and seeing the other black still in dreamland. he, exclaims: -

"Say, boss, nunga lazy mucka waijela!" (Say, boss. lazy blackfellow, no good to white man!)

"Weir tired pfella!" (No, he's a tired fellow).

"An-gool-a-jing ill-a shift 'em!" (I'll walk close up and shift him!)

With this, Tommy goes off, and returns very soon after with an axe in his hand, remarking, "Nunga full sleep, me wake 'em close up!" Saying this, he vigorously attacks with his axe the small tree under which Jacky is sleeping. Jacky woke with a start, and had hardly time to wash the dirt out of his eyes and bound away before the tree crashed down. Tommy, quite satisfied now at seeing Jacky on his feet, calmly resumes work, saying nothing, but thinking a deuce of a lot.

The blacks imitate the whites wherever possible, and, moreover, they respect the customs of the whites. For instance, when the wild blacks come into Ooldea, they are costumed in the clothing fashionable in their country, i.e, nil. But they are no sooner in camp that the older inhabitants fix them up with any old clothing. A recent arrival from the Everard Ranges, away to the north, was given a pair of trousers, and he endeavored to put them on in imitation of the white paragon. In the first attempt he tried to put them on over his head, but not being successful, he was informed that the legs must go in first. Trying this, he put one leg in all right, but then turned the trousers back to front. That not succeeding, he made other attempts, but failed in each, and giving it up as a bad job, and amid the shrieks of laughter from the other blacks, he dashed away behind some bushes to ponder over the intricacies of the white man's garment.

There have been instances where imitation of the whites, combined with the curiosity which is natural in the blacks, has been disastrous to them. One case is on record out here where a black had secured a rifle, and after loading it in quite correct white-man fashion, he looked down the barrel to see where the bullet was. Another black, equally inquisitive, tried the trigger. The grave of the other chap was just three feet deep.

Another black, observing how easily game was killed by a gun, was induced to have a shot. In true white-man style he raised the gun to his shoulder, took aim, and pressed the trigger. Immediately he felt the kick, he threw the gun into the air and cut for his life, under the impression that he had been shot. The interested group of black (and white) spectators enjoyed the joke immensely.

One evening we were having a social in the Progress Hall, when our dusky friends made an appearance, and they were invited inside just as. a phonograph was being made ready for playing. After the operator had explained to them that "debil-debil" was inside the box, the blacks were lined up in front and the instrument was set playing. A panic among the blacks immediately ensued, amid roars of laughter from the whites, and they bolted from the room. No amount of coaxing would bring them back until the nungas (i.e., the men) had prepared for battle. Thus fortified with the nullah, the sling and the spear, they approached within a few yards of the instrument, and the music was again started. The blacks again made a hurried retreat, some leaving their weapons behind. However, "curiosity killed the cat," and back they came. It was some little time before the phonograph was opened and the works exposed. The blacks were intensely delighted at the destruction of the "debil-debil," and when they saw the joke, they laughed boisterously, and later contributed to the evening's entertainment with a song and dance. And now the phonograph is a great favorite with the darkies, particularly the negro melodies. Who knows, but that in their mind's eye they can see Old Sambo strumming the banjo "way down in Tennessee."

A "new *chum" black, fresh in from the north, was offered an apple. As fruit was a mystery to him, he refused, but his dusky mate, who had once upon a time tasted of the forbidden fruit, said she would show him how to eat it, and so she took a large bite. Then she told her mate to have a bite, but he timidly took the smallest morsel. Then Polly had another bite, bigger than her first, and the rest of the apple disappeared into the cavern. The look of astonishment of her lord and master gave place to a hearty laugh as he realised from his mate's attitude how he had been taken in. Another apple was offered, and accepted; but the man from the Musgrave required no more teaching to show him how it should be eaten.

Mary's visit to the train was highly successful, and she found herself overwhelmed with choice morsels from the dining car - fruits, biscuits, "'bacca," etc. etc. These, as she received them, were placed on the ground, but the accumulation was such that she was sorely puzzled as to how she was to take the delicacies alonga camp. Mary waited for the train to depart and then thinking she would be a Lady Godiva, she took off her dress, wrapped the food up in it, slung the parcel over her shoulder, and went off alonga camp as happy as Larry.

The telegraph is an unfathomable mystery to the blacks, and whilst they know that white men communicate with each other by that means, they cannot understand how it is done. To settle an argument which arose among the blacks concerning this marvel, a deputation was appointed to make enquiries from me, and the leader of the deputation was inclined to be just a little cheeky. The spokesman asked, "Did 'debil-debil' make message?" "Oo- ah! (Oh, yes!) big fella debil-debil all bite 'em up quick! You like feel 'em, eh?" "Oo-ah!" "Well, catch 'em here and here!" So saying, I got each in turn to put their fingers on the two points of contact, the current having been previously switched off. After all had tried, and, of course, without experiencing anything, I got them all to join hands, and then for each end man to place his hand on a contact point. Immediately they did so, I switched on the current, and then there was a wild yell, a wilder rush, some heels showing through the dust, and I was alone with the silence.

Ask a black about the "telegraph debil-debil," and you'll find he has no desire to speak about it, but, on account of my power over this evil spirit, I am held in a great deal of respect, perhaps of awe.

It is well known to us out here that the blacks derive more fun from the passengers than do the passengers from them. On one occasion a passenger tried to work off before some fellow-voyagers a joke at the expense of a black, but the latter's skilful reply roused a hearty laugh from the other blacks and from the white passengers. This is what passed: -

The Passenger: "Look at the flies: aren't they awful? Plenty flies around here, Jacky."

The Nunga: "Muck a (no) fly until you come."

A black came into possession of a watch. With chest stuck out he came strutting along among the other blacks proudly displaying the timepiece. Every now and then he would have a look at the watch and nod his head, as much as to say, "Yes, it's all right!" A stranger, quite convinced that the black understood the watch, asked him to tell "the time." Tommy proudly pulled out his watch, the other blacks looking on in admiration, and scrutinising the watch this way and then that, he gravely replied, with the back of the watch facing him. "Time!" The other blacks could hear the ticking, and Tommy had told the time. All were very proud of his achievement.

A dog belonging to a black killed one of our fowls, and Micky was suspected of ownership of the culprit. "Now Micky," I said, "Mucka (no) tell 'em lie. That dog been yours?" "Mucka," said Micky, "that pfella Tommy's." "Now, now," I replied, "I see 'em that dog alonga you mission station!" "Oo-ah (yes) boss, that plenty right. My dog go alonga mission station. I lose him then; no good me!" "Ah, why lose 'em then?" "Well," answered Micky, "When dog start go church, mucka (no) good Micky. I give 'em Tommy!"

A hungry black approached one of our women folk and said: "Me hungry pfella, no sleep 'em last night. You got 'em cold tea?" The lady replied, "Hungry are you? I think 'em lazy fellow too!" "Mucka (no) lazy pfella, me boss." "Oh, boss are you? Well cut some wood, then get cold tea," she answered. "Boss pfella mucka (no) work like that!" he naively replied. "Well," she said, "No cut wood, no get tea." "Oo-ah, mucka wood; hungry plenty, but not all finish up yet." He was desperately hungry, but not sufficiently so that he had to cut wood.

Finding a dingo missing from a trap in which it had been presumably caught, and suspecting a black of having taken it, one of our men said to the suspect: "You tell 'em me quick which fellow take 'em dingo alonga trap!" The artful scamp replied, "Mucka (not) me, boss, I never been see 'em, true!" "Didn't you? Well, which nunga (blackfellow) take 'em then?" "Truly," said the black, "me no see 'em pup-pah (dingo)!" "No?" said the white, "well, you been out alonga my trap; what for, eh?" "Mucka me; I been walk about spear 'em gib-arra (turkey)." The white, seeing that he could get no admission from the black, resorted to magic, and assuming anger, he said, "Big fellow get wild, pull 'em out teeth, quick," and so saying he put his fingers into his mouth. The whites of the nunga's eyes began to show prominently, clearly indicating that he was getting frightened. After many frantic efforts and grimaces out come the white man's false teeth, and with these in his hand he approaches the black, who thoroughly frightened, bursts out: "Yarrie's dog been caught 'em alonga your trap. Him mucka (would not) steal dog; only let 'em go. True pfella me, boss!"

A young black was greatly interested in a particular book owned by one of our kiddies, and he would often ask for it, saying "Book, show 'em me!" On receiving it, away he would go, and soon would be laughing heartily. On one occasion he was showing the book to some other blacks, and they were in roars of laughter. My curiosity being aroused, I peeped over their heads to see the cause, and found that they were looking at an illustration of a kangaroo chasing a dog. "Ha, ha, ha! Mucka (no) catch 'em yet; close up two week now!" The kangaroo had been chasing the dog for the past two weeks and had not caught him, and the black had been looking at the book each day to see how things were going.

A black having borrowed a muzzle-loader, was being instructed as to loading it. "Now, Tommy, put in powder first time, then paper like this (illustrating the action), then shot, then more paper, see?" Tommy replied 'Yes, I see 'em all right boss. Plenty shoot, by-by." Tommy went away fully equipped; and was absent for several days. When he did show up, he was minus the gun. "Where's my gun?" said the irate owner. "Dunno," Tommy answered, pouting his lips and pointing away "I lose 'em. I been load 'em all right boss. Put powder, then shirt; then more powder, then more shirt, then more powder, then more shirt; then hold 'em up like this (imitating the action of shooting), then pull. Yes boss, kangaroo he go that way; me go this way; gun he go hell plenty. Me been lose 'em."

When the train pulled up a flash young fellow, jingling silver in his pocket, alighted and addressed a black boy thus: "Say boy, can you buy papers here?" "Oo-ah! (yes), close-up store," replied the black, pointing to the store. "Er, ha, Adelaide paper? eh?" "Oo-ah, plenty paper alonga store!" "Here, get me one" (giving the black a shilling). Jimmy went off to the store, and returned soon afterwards with a small packet which, to the general laugh of all around, he handed to the toff. He had brought back a packet of cigarette papers.

A scientific lady was very anxious to see the markings on an old black's leg, and thus addressed him: "Hullo, Joe, you show 'em me mark alonga leg?" The old man replied "Mucka (no)! What you been see 'em for, eh?" "Oh," answered the lady in an off-hand manner, "just to see if look like mine, Joe." "Oo-ah," retorted the black, "you been show 'em me first time!" That ended it; Joe wanted to see her leg first; then he would show his. There was no leg-show that day.

The Premier of Western Australia, when journeying to the Treasurer's Conference in Melbourne recently, heard at Ooldea a story that greatly amused him. A week or so earlier a prominent member of the Western Australian Legislature, noted for his beneficence, was among the passengers who, at the historic watering place for blacks and the explorers, descended from the train to stretch their limbs. The scantiness of the attire worn by one lubra either shocked the sense of decency or appealed to the altruistic in the legislator, and in full view of everybody, he took off his shirt, and handed it to "the lady in black," exhorting her to put it on. She disappeared, and the train went on. Next day the lubra was challenged by one of the local authorities to account for the possession of a garment bearing in legible characters a name well-known in Western Australia. "Him gib it me!" explained the artless lady. Then with a flash of feminine inspiration she proceeded-"Him my man! Me Mrs!"

A black was very inquisitive as to starting the engine of a motor car that came up from the coast. Seeing the chauffeur turning the handle, he asked - "This one turn 'em make 'em go plenty?" and got the reply "Yes, turn that round and off she goes!" "Oo-ah, what you call 'em that one?" (pointing to the crank). "White fellow call that 'engine crank.'" The black then asked "Moto' go plenty by crank eh?"; and then, being puzzled at the general laugh which his question created, he added quickly "Me think 'em all cranky, all same moto' crank!"

As the black moves off for his evening meal he frequently fires the parting shot "I come along supper time get 'em cold tea." Long before supper time the black is sitting outside the window waiting. We do not recognise his presence. We hear a cough, but take no notice. A little later two coughs; yet still we "no hear 'em." Another spell, then three coughs louder than the previous ones; we might be deaf for all the notice we take. Yet another silence, then all at once "bang!" goes a tin on the ground. Looking out the door, innocently we remark, "Hullo Jacky, you here, are you'" "Oo-ah (yes)," replied the sable one, "me been drop 'em billy-can; plenty noise; no tea inside! You been got 'em cold tea, eh?" There was no tea, eh?" There was no tea in the billy when he dropped it, consequently it made a loud noise; with tea inside there would have been no noise.

The blacks are very fond of looking at picture books,
more particularly those containing illustrations of animals. One day Sambo asked for the children's "zoo" book; and whenever he came across the picture of an animal he had not seen before, he would ask our children the name. The following conversation took place on one occasion: -
Black: "What this one, Bubby?"
Bubby: "That one, Elephant!"
Black: "Balya boolga!" (good, big).
Black: (seeing kangaroo); "Ought Mar-leu!"; then coming across one he did not know, "What this one, Bubby?"
Bubby: "Lion."
Black: "Oo-ah, me bin see 'em alonga train" (when Wirth's circus passed through). Looking at the Elephant again he says, "That one balya!" (good).
Bubby: "You like that one, Sambo?"
Black: "Elephant balya, mucka tail, no good. Mar-leu tail," then, "boolga balya!" (The elephant was "good-oh"; but Sambo did not like the little tail. Put the kangaroo's tail on that elephant, then that would suit the elephant splendidly.)

The blacks do not conceal their emotions, excepting when there is necessity. Disgust or disdain is not repressed, as the following will show. When Sir Harry Lauder was travelling along the Trans-Australian Railway after the completion of one of his "final" tours of Australia, he was interested in the blacks, and on arrival at Ooldea he selected one who he thought looked intelligent, and plied him with questions. The natives had heard the railway men say that Sir Harry Lauder was coming by the train. Although the kilt was a matter of interest to the black, and caused him to remark later on, "Wil-ba plenty that pfella, all same us" (wind blows about that fellow the same as it does to us), he took no notice of Sir Harry's questions, but kept looking up and down the train, as if anxious to see some person. Sir Harry moved on to find a native more responsive to his inquiries. The black then turned to his mates, and asked, "Which one big pfella white man?" On Sir Harry being pointed out to him, he remarked, "Bah! him no speak 'em all same white pfella!" And then, in a disdainful tone he added, "Him silly old woman!" Sir Harry's burr and his kilt did not apparently impress the man from the Musgrave.

A black seeing me wearing a watch, asks me if I would sell it to him. "You been sell 'em me watch?" said he. "Mucka," said I; "what you want 'em watch for?" "Me tell 'em time!" boasted he, and to which I replied, "You can't tell 'em time?" "Oo-ah (yes)!" "Well, what is the time now by the watch?" queried I. Looking at the watch he proudly said, "This one dinner time!" illustrating his remark by placing two fingers, one on top of the other over the XII figure on the watch. "This one supper time!" continued he, pointing at the figures VI. with his two fingers placed end on. He certainly could tell the time by the watch, and I guess he would never be late for meals!

When the blacks come into the neighborhood of the whites they put on any old clothes that may be about, but they quickly cast them aside when they leave the camp, or when the whites go away. This casting-off of clothing frequently results in the blacks catching a cold. Once when a mild epidemic of influenza got the blacks in its grip some friendly disposed whites administered a few drops of kerosene as a cure. One old gin could on no account be persuaded to take the kerosene, and, after much coaxing she gave the reason for the refusal. "Well, why you no take 'em medicine?" she was asked. "That one mucka (not) medicine! By-by me smoke. Chunee (stomach) catch 'em fire! Medicine all burn up!" was her reply. When she lit her pipe the vapor from the kerosene would catch fire, and her stomach would be burnt up. Another instance of the cure being worse than the disease!

A gin had been rewarded for some slight service in one of our cottages, and she was asked what had been given to her. The following dialogue took place: -

White: What you been get 'em?

Black: Me been get 'em ea-ar.

White: What, get money?

Black: Mucka (not) money; ea-ar.

White: That one mucka (not) white fellow?

Black: Oo-ah (yes)! Cor-nil-datta; all same brother apple!

She could not say "peal," but she conveyed her meaning by calling it a "brother apple."

In the station office I have two typewriters, one an ordinary Underwood, the other a small portable machine of the same make. One day a black was intently looking at the big machine, when I asked, "Well, what you want?" He replied, "Mucka (no) want 'em. What pfella that one?" (pointing to the typewriter). "That pfella write 'em down talk, big pfella wonga!" I said; then bringing out the small machine I remarked "This one little talk!" The black asked, 'That juga-juga picaninny big one?" (That little one baby big one?) "Yes," I replied, amid shrieks of laughter. They suggested that the big machine had given birth to a baby one. I had a busy time afterwards showing the "juga-juga wonga" (little talker) to many inquiring blacks.

"Corroboree to-night, Bobby? " I asked.

"Might be," replied my friend.

"I see. Who dance 'em to-night?" I asked to make sure.

"I dunno. Might be Jimmy, Mickey, Jackie, I think 'em."

"When you finish 'em all up, eh?" I queried.

"Might be to-morrow,   might be close up: all finish by-bye," replied the ambiguous one.

"All finish by-and-bye, eh?" I said.

"Might be!" he replied.

One day a black noticed that the signals were "off," although it was not a usual train day, and on his enquiring as to the reason he was informed that a light engine was coming. Throughout the blacks' camp the news spread like wildfire that a curious small engine was coming. "White pfella call 'em 'light engine,'" they said. Imagine their digust when an ordinary engine duly arrived! One of them expressed the general opinion when he said, "Mucka light pfella, plenty boolga!" (Not a light engine, but a heavy one!).

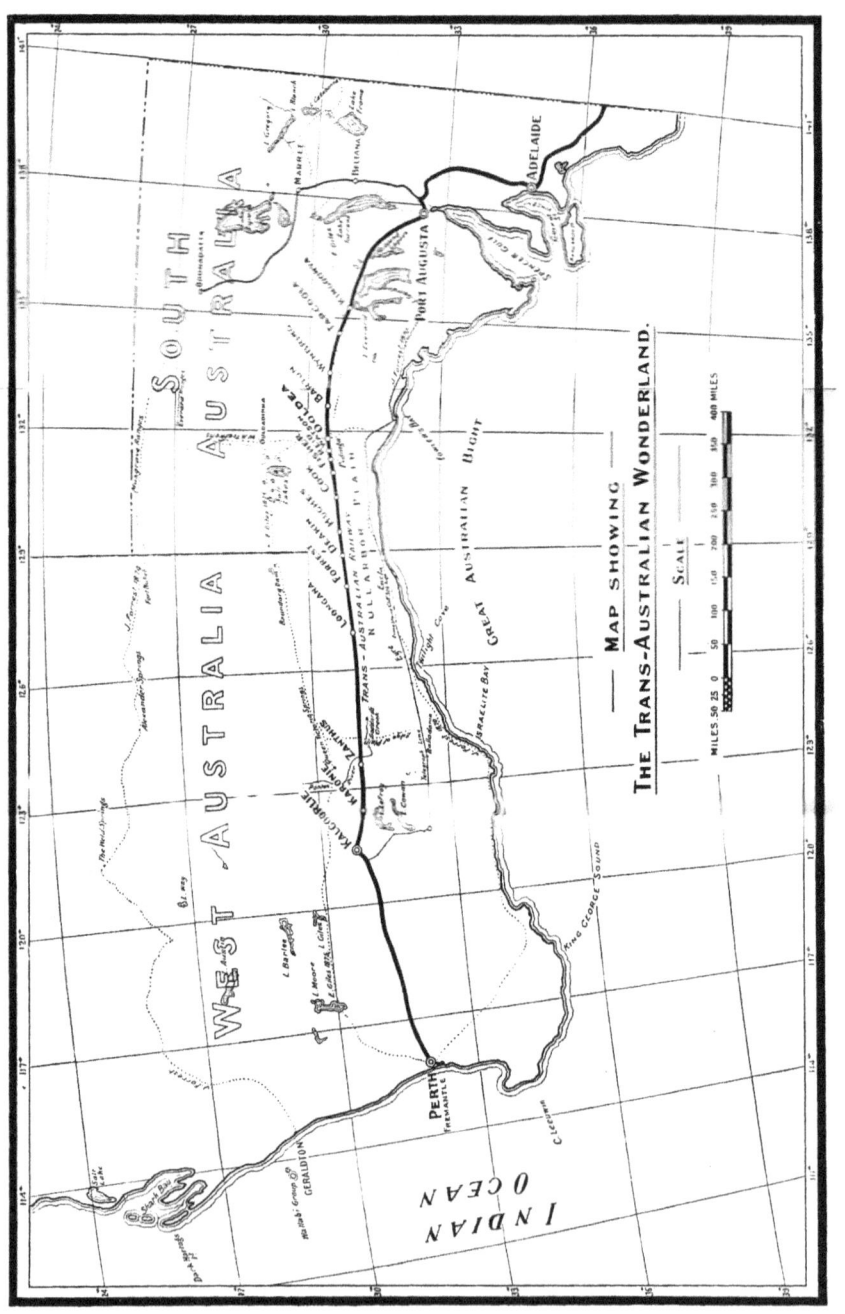

www.ingramcontent.com/pod-product-compliance
Lightning Source LLC
Chambersburg PA
CBHW030942090426
42737CB00007B/501